THE ALPHABET
OF MANLINESS

THE ALPHABET OF MANLINESS

MADDOX

Illustrations by

Angelo Vildasol
Bryan Douglas
Jim Moore
John Petersen
Justina Fader
Leah Tiscione
Louis Fernet-Leclair
Thomas Pollock Jr.

CITADEL PRESS
Kensington Publishing Corp.
www.kensington.com

CITADEL PRESS BOOKS are published by

Kensington Publishing Corp.
850 Third Avenue
New York, NY 10022

All Kensington titles, imprints, and distributed lines are available at special quantity discounts
for bulk purchases for sales promotions, premiums, fund-raising, educational, or institutional
use. Special book excerpts or customized printings can also be created to fit specific needs. For
details, write or phone the office of the Kensington special sales manager: Kensington
Publishing Corp., 850 Third Avenue, New York, NY 10022, attn: Special Sales Department;
phone 1-800-221-2647.

CITADEL PRESS and the Citadel logo are Reg. U.S. Pat. & TM Off.

First printing: June 2006

10 9 8

Printed in the United States of America

Library of Congress Control Number: 2005934013

ISBN 0-8065-2720-X

To the love of my life, my soul mate,
and the greatest person in the world: Me

FOREWORD

It's 5 AM and I'm editing a picture of a Shaolin Monk to make it look like he's head-butting a small child. Earlier, I received an e-mail with the subject line: "go fuck yourself"; it's from someone who just read my website for the first time. The sender goes on to call me a "pathetic virgin" and a "homo." He ends the e-mail by saying that he prays that I get cancer.

My name is Maddox, and I'm the author of the website "The Best Page in the Universe." My site started out as my personal homepage back in 1997, and since then it has amassed a following of millions of readers by word-of-mouth alone. Ever wonder where all those e-mail forwards that your friends send you come from? Me neither. Nevertheless, some of the content comes from me. I don't send the e-mails to you, but my material gets passed around anyway, until several months later someone will forward a copy of my own work back to me, telling me to "check out what this asshole wrote." It's flattering at first, until someone accuses me of plagiarizing myself.

One thing that separates my site from the majority of others is that I don't have advertisements, pop-ups, epileptic spasm banners, or any other obnoxious bullshit that makes the Internet unbearable. Not having advertisements has allowed me to say whatever I want without self-censorship, but it comes at a tremendous cost to me. I'm giving up $12,000 a month to bring my site to the masses, censorship and annoyance free. Not only that, but the bandwidth it takes to host my site costs more than most people's mortgage payments.

So after running the site for free all these years, you're probably wondering why am I publishing a book now? Simple: money. I want as much money as possible. I want to go to exclusive Hollywood parties where I'll feel in place using the word "amazing" as a noun. I want some serious "fuck you" money. I want to be so rich that instead of having my henchmen kill people, I can do it myself in broad daylight in front of the Chief Justice of the Supreme Court, while I download music illegally from the Internet. Also, not having to eat ramen soup ever again would be nice.

The other question you're probably wondering is "What does Maddox know about manliness?" To answer your question, I would refer you to the hair on my knuckles. And if that weren't enough, I'd show you the hair on my back. I didn't wear a shirt to work for an entire month one time and nobody noticed.

ABOUT THE BOOK

This book is all about men and what men like. It's the definitive reference book about manliness. If it needs to be shaved, beaten, or sexed, there's a good chance it'll be in this book. Everything from the classy bible-like filigree on the front cover to the diagrams and tabs on each page give this book a frank and authoritative feel. If you're standing around in a bookstore with your thumb up your ass, wondering why someone would have a picture of a man punching a gorilla on the cover of a book, this book isn't for you. Kindly put it down and get the fuck out of the store. On the other hand, maybe you're a woman and you're reading this wondering "Is this book just for men?" I would say that it is only for men in the same way that lesbian porn sites on the Internet are only for women.

ACKNOWLEDGMENTS

This is the part in books where I usually skim the names in the off chance that somebody mentioned me, as you are undoubtedly doing now. I'm always disappointed when I don't get mentioned, so I did my best not to leave anyone off the long list of people who helped make this book possible.

First and foremost, I would like to thank Cherry for putting up with my ill-temperament, grumpiness, and general bullshit while I wrote this book. She has been the most supportive person throughout this entire process, experiencing many of the same hardships that I experienced in seeing this book to its end. She tirelessly gave me advice and feedback at all hours of the day, even during my 5 AM red-eye sessions. Her understanding and tolerance knows no bounds. It's not possible to overstate her importance in writing this book. There would be no book without her, and that's no joke.

I know I sound like a shit stabber by saying "thanks to all my fans," but really, thanks to all my fans who have supported me, sent me amusing e-mail, porn, viruses, or signed me up to spam lists over the years. It's been a blast deleting all your e-mails. Really, though, thanks for spreading the word and checking my site even in between infrequent updates. I'd especially like to thank everyone at the fan sites "Maddox Mania, The Best Fan Page in the Universe," and my fans on IRC for their dedication. Without you assholes, none of this would be possible.

Next, I would like to thank my editor, Jeremie Ruby-Strauss, for all his hard work and enthusiasm for this project. He's by far one of the most straightforward and honest guys I've ever had the pleasure of dealing with; he just plain tells it like it is. Jeremie first contacted me over four years ago, and persisted until I finally got a deal. He adapts to emerging talents and technologies, and is one of the few people out there who truly "gets it."

Several of my friends were especially helpful in writing this book by reading early drafts and spending countless hours giving me advice and feedback at late night coffee shops: Dan "Taskmaster" Berman for his tremendous support and input. He kept me in line when I was on the verge of burning out and inserted gay porn into my manuscript to make sure I was paying attention. Dan and I collaborated on several sections in this book, and I'm very grateful for his help (check out his site at DanBerman.com). I also have to thank Tim Baker for his always lively commentary, solid advice, and for his very quick response to my initial draft. Thanks to Robert and Jamie D'Ausilio for their input, support, and encouragement over the years. My family for making this world a better place by having me.

Thanks to Robert Hamburger for paving the way for authors such as myself. Without the success of his book, *Real Ultimate Power*, many authors like me wouldn't have ever been given a chance. My Internet service provider, Xmission (xmission.com), for their excellent service and anti-censorship policy that has allowed my site to stay up for over nine years and counting. Curtiss Lopez and Erin Tyler for their help with the cover layout. Justin Killion for his friendship, enthusiasm and input with several sections of this book. My good friend Shawn Schepps for imparting me with her sage-like wisdom over the years. Tamara Thorne for her very helpful advice and insight. She's not only a talented author, but knows her way around a DOS prompt. Michael Gross from the Author's Guild (authorsguild.org) for his enormous help with the technical details. My book agent, Howard Yoon, for helping me with the contract negotiations and his forthrightness.

I'd like to thank my illustrators for their phenomenal work and the utmost professionalism. I know it can be hard to remain professional when asked to draw pictures of snowmen made out of tits and pirates ejaculating leprechauns, but they really came through when I needed them. Many of my illustrators stayed up late, worked weekends, and some even worked holidays to help get this project done. I couldn't have asked for a better crew to work with. These illustrators were all fans of my site before they were selected for this project, and I think their enthusiasm for this project shines through in their work. It was difficult choosing just 8 of the 762 potential candidates, and after seeing the submissions I received, I know for a fact that I have the most talented readers on the Internet.

Thanks to the staff at Kensington for dealing with my delays. This book turned out to be a lot more work than I originally expected. I would also like to mention Tucker Max, Max Wong, Carl, Chuck Norris, my close friends Andy, Dan, Erik, Mike, Robert, and Roy for their encouragement, support, or influence over the years. Also, thanks to the staff at Cup of Joe, and the dude who works late shifts at the 7-11 down the street for their coffee-related services.

But most of all, I'd like to thank me. Without me, none of this would have been possible. I really did a bang-up job on this book, and I deserve all the credit. I hereby revoke all the gratitude I expressed above and keep it for myself.

THE ALPHABET
OF MANLINESS

is for...
ASS-KICKING

THE PHRASE "ASS KICKING" has changed over the years from its humble origin as the union of one's foot with another person's ass, to an expression today that has nothing to do with asses, or even kicking. The picture at the beginning of this section epitomizes ass kicking. Time for a pop quiz: What's more awesome than a lumberjack punching Santa in the face? (A) Nothing, or (B) All the above. I gave this quiz to my friend's wife, and she got the wrong answer. She kept asking questions like "what's so cool about Santa getting punched in the face? That's not cool, that's mean."

Figure 1: Ass, meet foot

Wrong answer, bitch. The reason she doesn't "get it" is the same reason all women don't get it: Men invented ass kicking along with chainsaws, beef jerky, and happiness.

Although purists would agree that the classic ass kicking (Figure 1) is sufficiently awesome and/or tits, new approaches, techniques, and interpretations have been welcomed to the ass-kicking catalogue over the years. Take for example the punch-to-the-cojones ass kicking. Just follow the two simple steps in Figures 2 and 3 to find yourself ball-busting in no time.

THE COCK PUNCH

There are two main procedures for transferring one's fist to the cock. The first method is the crescent punch, which is especially handy with missionaries who can't take a hint, people who jog in place while waiting for the light to turn green, and self-important clerks who ask, "What can I do you for?" Of course, if you answer the subtle sexual proposition, the clerk will always seem confused because it's a mantra that's often chanted unintentionally, almost like it's a desperate last attempt at being a comedian, or anything else that doesn't so closely resemble the mundane hell of life in a convenience store, thus warranting a slug to said clerk's pecker. The crescent approach isn't a cock punch in the strictest sense of the word, as one rarely punches the actual cock as defined as shaft + helmet. It's more of a nut busting (not to be confused with busting a nut), but still, it's related to the cock punching family.

CRESCENT METHOD

STEP 1: Wind back in a graceful, semicircular motion (Figure 2). Note: the trick here is having a good excuse to find yourself below the victim's waist line. For example, try saying "oops, I need to tie my shoe laces," or "hey look, some spare change," or the fail safe "I think I'll crouch down here for no reason, especially not to punch you in the dick."

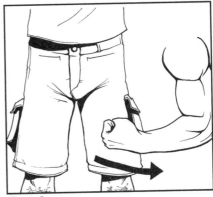

Figure 2

STEP 2: Thrust your fist into the opponent's crotch so that the momentum of your thrust is directed upward, as if to force the gonads back into the pelvic cavity (Figure 3). Note: if your victim happens to be a woman, this method is known as the "ovarian delight," which isn't a delight so much as a jab to the ovaries.

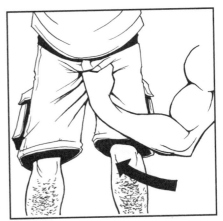

Figure 3

STEALTH METHOD

The second, more common delivery method is the top-down, or high-level approach. It is sometimes referred to as the "stealth" method because the victim rarely foresees the dong thumping he's about to receive. This method is most easily carried out during casual conversations, especially as a substitute for feigning interest in whatever boring activity your co-workers filled their weekends with.

Figure 4: Let him know you mean business with a stealthy jab to the shaft.

Start out with a friendly gesture, perhaps a bit of light small talk like "how's it going?" Or even "hanging in there?" Don't get too carried away though. Asking questions like "how's work?" might suggest that you have some knowledge of whatever project your co-worker is working on, which might give him or her the impression that you're interested, or even worse, that you care.

If things go awry and you find yourself inundated with too much boring psychobabble too quickly, it's acceptable to initiate early, though a premature thrust may dampen the satisfaction of leading your victim on with knowing nods and polite "mmm hmm"s. When you're finally ready, make sure to step into the punch so you have the weight of your body backing you (Figure 4). If you punch hard enough, it's possible to punch someone's dick clean off, though you have to be extremely manly to do this. We're talking hairy eyeballs.

DROPKICK TO THE FACE

The dropkick isn't just for impressing your peers by dispatching litter into a ravine, or for those unfortunate occasions when you find yourself actually having to play soccer. The dropkick can be employed in situations ranging from setting a friend straight for making eye contact at a urinal to punishing children for bad grades.[1]

Figure 5

STEP 1: Hold the subject by his head (Figure 5).

STEP 2: While standing on one foot, lift one of your legs back to charge for the kick, and simultaneously drop your subject (Figure 6). Caution: It is important to note here that you must drop the subject. Do not toss him! This is a dropkick, not some pansy tosskick (Figure 7). Do it right, don't be an asshole.

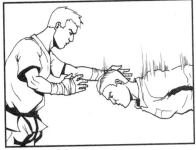

Figure 6: Right

Figure 7: Fucking wrong.

STEP 3: Connect the kick with the face. As awesome as this is, try to stay focused to make it count (Figure 8). You may optionally gloat, but do not initiate some stupid Super Bowl touchdown dance. This will only make you look stupid, which may qualify you for a cock punch of your own.

Figure 8

1. Or good grades, depending on your mood.

PLAIN OLD HONEST-TO-GOD PUNCH TO THE MOUTH

Sometimes a friend or relative will do or say something so stupid that you have no choice but to cock your arm back and slug that son of a bitch right in the mouth. Sometimes the person is so annoying that this happens involuntarily, like your arms transform into sentient beings with a primal sense of justice, lashing out at the source of your frustration like a reflex; nothing too showy, just a plain old-fashioned punch to the kisser (Figure 9).

For example, everyone knows someone who will drive an extra ten minutes across town to buy gas from a station selling its fuel for $.01 per gallon cheaper than other gas stations. For 99 percent of the population, it's obvious why this is stupid, but for the rest of you who don't understand why it's a waste of time (i.e., the two or three women who will get this far into the book), I'll elaborate: the average car can hold fifteen gallons per tank, so if you save $.01 per gallon, that's $0.15 you save every time you fill up, which is usually once per week for most people. So that means you'll save $0.60 per month, or $7.20 per year. If the average person drives from the age of sixteen to sixty-five, that's forty-nine years of driving, which brings your grand total of lifetime savings to: $dick.

When you point this out to your frugal acquaintance, he will ramble on for hours with various precalculated scenarios designed to save him a trivial amount of pocket change. What these tight-fisted misers don't realize is the amount of money they could save by not having to buy extra food to restore the countless calories of energy they expel by simply not shutting the fuck up about how much money they save on gasoline.

These are the same people who consider it a wise investment of their time to undertake the laborious task of pouring over newspapers

Figure 9

on the off chance of finding a coupon for a product that they want—let alone need. You see these people everywhere: haggling over the price of candy at checkout counters, sending back steaks that don't live up to their epicurean standards at Red Lobster, and bringing commerce to a grinding halt by tediously writing out every letter of every number on their checks. No man pays with checks. Real men pay for things with real money. Slabs of molded ore if possible, and if not, then with big crumpled wads of lint-caked bills, straight from our swampy pockets to the register. Cut the foreplay; you give us stuff, we give you money; end of transaction. None of this organized memo-field bullshit. If you need a memo to remind you of what you spent your money on, then you probably shouldn't be buying it in the first place. Stick to the basics.

Speaking of basics, as straightforward as a punch to the mouth can be, it's not as efficient as it could be at delivering the ass kicking.

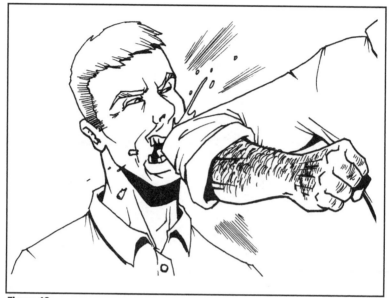

Figure 10

The fewer joints involved in pummeling someone, the less likely it will be that one of the joints will bend incorrectly, which could dampen a blow. A more direct approach would be to forego the wrist joint entirely. In other words, cut the middleman and go right to the elbow.

MOUTH FULL OF ELBOW

Hitting someone in the mouth with your elbow requires close proximity to your target. One of the few occasions that you might get close enough to someone to make a delivery is when you're talking to a friend or a relative.

You might be hesitant at first to pummel a friend, but here's a thought: by not hitting your close acquaintances, you're discriminating against them. What kind of friend discriminates? Show him that you're a true friend by giving him a taste of your elbow (Figure 10).

HEAD-BUTT TO THE OVARIES

Sometimes a woman will manipulate a man with her striking good looks and flirtatious demeanor. This type of woman can live her entire life without lifting a finger to earn a penny; instead, she opts to lead men on with a life that can best be described as one long cock tease of an existence. Since it's unbecoming of a man to hit a woman,[2] sometimes a guy needs to find another method to keep her in line. Sometimes a man needs to head-butt a woman in the ovaries.

The head-butt is tricky to maneuver since there are very few reasons a guy should ever find himself kneeling in front of a woman. One potentially legitimate reason a woman might expect to find a guy on his knees is for a proposal—which is clichéd and stupid, but play along. Just get on one knee and reach into your pocket like you're going to pull out a ring. Then when she least expects it, grab her thighs, buck your head back (Figure 11), and thrust your forehead into her baby maker (Figure 12).

Figure 11: Take a firm grasp of her legs to catch her off guard.

Figure 12: Bam! Right in the ovaries!

BACK BREAKER

Tired of foreplay? Want to tell a certain someone "I'm not working late this weekend, so you can kiss my black ass" in not so many

2. Unless she's a feminist, in which case aggression toward her would be a sign of respect, since feminists want to be treated with equality.

ASS-KICKING

words—or no words at all? The back breaker is a great alternative and will assert your manliness like few other ass kicking methods will.

To break someone's back, you have all the tools you need on your body: hands and knees. Here's how:

STEP 1: Take hold of your opponent and lift him in the air above your head. Make sure to do this dramatically, like a professional wrestler would (Figure 13).

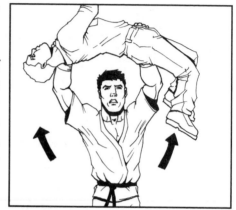

Figure 13

STEP 2: Drop on one knee so that your other leg is extended outward, then thrust your victim down onto your out-stretched knee so that the center of his lower back takes the brunt of your thrust (Figure 14). You may now make a formal declaration that his shit has been ruined.

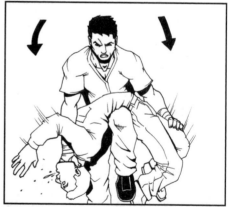

Figure 14

Note: after administering the back breaker, your victim won't be able to walk, so you may get cited for littering if you leave him lying in the street.

 is for...
BONERS

CONTRARY TO POPULAR BELIEF and empirical evidence, every male child is born with an erection. While nobody knows what causes this phenomenon, there are some theories: some men get wood when they see naked women, while others—like me—sprout a big rubbery one while watching chicks fight. In fact, just the other day I saw some chick getting kicked in the crotch by another chick. It was the hottest thing I had ever seen, and before I knew it: *bam!* I popped a giant, life-threatening boner, with which I could easily crush a woman or bludgeon a small child.

BONERS

Doctors have been trying to explain boners away for years, with theories about blood flowing into penile tissue, blah blah blah. Too bad these theories don't explain why boners are so awesome. Men love getting boners, and by "getting," I mean "giving." I once dated a girl who was super pissed because I was an hour late for dinner; when I finally arrived, I told her that I brought her a gift. Naturally she put the shitstorm on hold and asked me what it was. Then POW: I suddenly sprung a tent in my pants, and she became so horny that she banged me right in the restaurant.

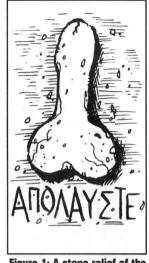

Figure 1: A stone relief of the sacred beef.

Throughout history, men have been giving boners to people on all occasions, but mostly birthdays and weddings (Figure 1). Take ancient Rome for example. It was customary for

Figure 2: A club-like boner: suitable for wallops.

men of the time to give a giant mural of themselves, fully engorged, to women as a sign of sexual potency and to other men as a threat of possible injury. A larger penis naturally meant a greater threat, and just like today, men rarely exaggerated their penis length in accordance with an unspoken penile code (Figure 2).

Men not only love their blood sausages, but they feel obligated to show their units to as many people as possible, as often as possible. For example, ever been to a wedding where they have hundreds of disposable cameras laying around for all the guests to take pictures with? As any man who has made the mistake of inviting guys to such a wedding knows, roughly 50 percent of all pictures taken by males at the party will be of their genitals dipped in the punch bowl and/or various people. In fact, I have a boner right now, and I would love nothing more than to ruin a friend's wedding photos with my juvenile dick jokes.

IS THERE A WRONG TIME TO POP A BONER?

Generally speaking, no. But things can get complicated during dentist appointments, funerals, and job interviews. I was at an interview one time, and as I was describing myself to the interviewer, I got carried away with how awesome I am, and before I knew it, I was fully aroused. So what to do if you sprout a chubby at an inopportune time? Sometimes all you can do is wait it out, but until then, you need some good cover.

CONCEALING A BONER

There are two ways to conceal a boner: the wrong way and the right way. Which method you choose depends on whether or not you're comfortable letting other people know that the cadaver isn't the only stiffy at the funeral.

Figure 3: Why is this jackass bent over? Busted.

THE WRONG WAY

The wrong way (Figure 3) to conceal a

boner almost isn't worth mentioning, because all men have tried it, and all men know it doesn't work. The method is simple: just bend over. The problem with this technique is that bending over draws attention to you. You might as well stand on a chair and shout, "Hey, look at me, I'm a fucking psycho."

Figure 4: The right way to conceal a boner.

THE RIGHT WAY

The right way (Figure 4) to conceal a boner is to cover it up with something. A newspaper, a jacket, or a family pet will do. If you don't have anything to cover it with, try going on the offensive when confronted. If a woman inquires, subtly suggest that perhaps she wants to be boned—in the butt. Despite a woman's natural inclination toward boners, most women will find this proposition too direct and will not inquire further. If a guy inquires, simply use the following two-step procedure to diffuse the situation.

STEP 1: Tell him that it just happens to be the way your pants bunch up in the crotch area when you sit down. It's not unusual for pants to do this, so it's a perfectly reasonable explanation.

STEP 2: Run.

BONER CORRELATIONS

By now, you know how to hide a boner and when to give one as a gift, but did you know that popping a boner means different things depending on when you pop it? Think of it as a sexual preference barometer. Here is a quick reference guide:

POPPING A BONER DURING THIS OCCASION	MAKES YOU
Movies in which the women aren't predominantly naked	GAY
Movies in which the women aren't predominantly naked, but there are lots of explosions, people getting maimed and/or killed.	STRAIGHT
Shower in gym.	GAY
Seeing a naked woman.	STRAIGHT
Seeing a naked woman who doesn't shave.	GAY
Shopping for a gun.	STRAIGHT
Shopping for a gun with your buddy.	STRAIGHT
Shopping for a gun with your buddy while you hold each other's cocks.	GAY
On your eighteenth birthday.	BARELY LEGAL
During a sleepover.	BI-CURIOUS
While doing math.	ASEXUAL
While doing your math teacher.	HEROIC

BONER TIMELINE

60,500 BC – Man discovers his boner.

60,500 (TEN MINUTES LATER) – Man kills his first small animal using his boner as a blunt striking tool.

Figure 5: Prehistoric man's triumph over dinosaurs, thanks in no small part to boners.

60,000 – Man wipes out last dinosaur on earth (Figure 5).

334 – Alexander the Great invades Persia with a battalion of fully engorged men riding horses that are also fully engorged. The Persian army, found to be relatively impotent, was quickly overwhelmed.

6 AD – A child is born in China who is so well endowed that he comes to be known as Emperor Wang and rules the Hsin Dynasty with his terrible pork-sword.

1200 – Giant brick boners are built all around the European countryside. Not having much practical use, the boners are later transformed into windmills.

1478 – Leonardo da Vinci is commissioned by a wealthy Florentine businessman to paint the *Mona Lisa*. For years, art historians have speculated about the reason behind her mysterious smile, until newly discovered evidence became unearthed (Figures 6–7).

1661 – Since Corvettes haven't been invented yet, Louis XIV declares himself the absolute ruler of France to compensate for his small penis.

1891 – The zipper is invented. Crimes related to indecent exposure and public urination increase by 5000 percent.

1942 – Mahatma Gandhi arrested for admonishing British colonial occupation. I'm not sure, but I think "admonish" means to "flail penis wildly."

1945 – Adolf Hitler takes his life at the conclusion of World War II. Not boner related, but still relevant since

Figure 6: Mona Lisa's famous smile has baffled historians for ages.

Figure 7: This sketch was discovered tucked away in a notebook belonging to Leonardo's pupil, Melzi, depicting the famous scene from a different perspective, proving conclusively that the reason Mona Lisa is smiling is because she had her eye on Leonardo's rock-hard yogurt cannon.

he was generally considered the biggest dick in history.

1962 – The Cuban missile crisis brings the world to the brink of war, but concludes peacefully without a single missile being fired. Americans and Cubans simultaneously suffer the worst case of blue balls in history.

OTHER USES FOR BONERS

Although the primary use of a boner is still for buffing a woman's flesh lettuce, there are other less conventional, yet practical, uses that can be applied to everyday living. For example, did you know that boners could be used as reach extenders? You're in the kitchen eating a ham sandwich, when all of a sudden your wife comes in and asks you to hand her the keys sitting on the stool next to you. Rather than interrupting your meal to reach over and pass them to her, simply scoop the key ring onto your meat staff and swing it over to her face. She'll be so impressed by your penile fortitude that she'll cook you a steak when she comes home from work.

Here are a few other uses for that pragmatic pervert inside us all:

• **HAMMER:** The beauty of using your man-crank as a hammer is that the more you use it, the more effective it becomes. Every whack to the head of a nail makes your boner more and more calloused. The rougher it gets, the more easily you'll be able to drive a nail through a piece of wood, or your wood through a piece of ass. There are other ways to make your boner rougher, but most of them involve chronic masturbation with sandpaper.

Figure 8: Why waste your energy holding that cup when you have a perfectly good platform in front of you?

- **CUP HOLDER:** This can only be done by the manliest of men (Figure 8).

- **USE IT TO HIT THE SPACEBAR KEY:** Not many people realize that a boner is the perfect instrument to slam the spacebar key with. In fact, all the white space in this book is brought to you courtesy of my boner.

- **WAKEUP CALL:** Ever catch a buddy sleeping at his desk at work? A great way to wake him up would be to poke him in the ear with your dick. The best way to do this would be to threaten him for months in advance so that he thinks it's just a long-running gag and you won't really do it. Then when you actually do it one day, he'll know you're all business.

• **PROVIDES SHADE:** If you happen to have short friends, a boner is perfect for providing shade during a hot summer day. Just make sure to use sun block so that you don't get sunburn on your wang—unless you're hankering for a wicked case of dick chaff.

is for...
COPPING A FEEL

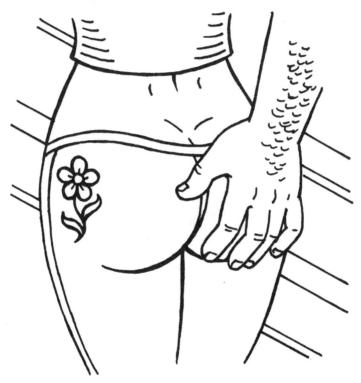

IN THE COURSE OF MANHOOD, every teenager will at some point be confronted with an unexpected opportunity to grope a woman. Given this situation, every budding man will have a choice to make: turn a blind eye to this bounty of gropeable flesh, or choose to do the inappropriate thing and cop a feel? The first instance may occur on a date, or while passing a woman in a tight corridor, or if you're especially perverse, while catching a woman falling

Figure 1: A damsel about to be distressed.

from a tree.[1] Think of it as a perk for your heroism, as all heroism deserves perks (Figure 1).

Finding the right moment to cop a feel requires delicate timing, expert maneuvering, and occasionally some social engineering. You don't want to seem too eager to touch a woman; don't just rush in and start grabbing like some rapist. That shit is annoying and looked down on by other men. Women also don't like it.

Take it easy on your first try. Go for a nonambitious target before you attempt to negotiate the finer points of the female anatomy. There's no shame in going for an obvious target when you're still learning.

---

1. You might be wondering "what would a woman be doing up a tree in the first place?" Without the guidance of men, women are known to wander aimlessly, and on occasion, find themselves in awkward places like trees, abandoned mine shafts, and, in some rare instances, even working for a living.

THE BUTT

A woman's posterior is the most grabbable part of her body, but first you must learn to find the right type of ass to grab. There's a great variety of asses out there, but unfortunately many of them aren't worth touching even in a clinical setting. The ideal type of woman for groping is a woman blessed with a thick ass. Don't confuse a "thick" ass for a fat ass (Figure 2). A fat ass is a sad ass. You don't want anything to do with a fat ass, other than to loathe it. A thick ass, on the other hand, is plump and beautiful; it should make you feel hungry like when you see a glazed ham that you can't afford in a Christmas catalogue (Figure 3). This is the

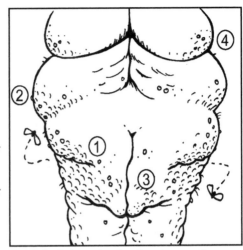

Figure 2: A droopy, pudgy, lumpy mess of an ass. Notice the pockmarks (1), awkwardly shaped slabs of meat jettisoning out from the sides of the waist (2), the clenched, uninviting crack (3), and the burgeoning folds of cellulite (4). Just nasty.

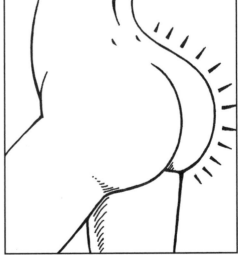

Figure 3: A thick ass looks like a happy smile. You can see that this ass is healthy and bursting with flavor.

best-case scenario for ass connoisseurs. You won't find a butt riper for the picking, so don't pass that ass.

Once you've found a suitable rear, now comes the tricky part: landing a grope without getting slapped, or better yet, without getting noticed. You'll find many opportunities to steal a feel, but sometimes the easiest opportunities are the best. Case in point: the hallway.

Hallways and narrow corridors are a perv's best friends. The trick to utilizing a hallway is to find yourself in close proximity to your subject—close enough that accidentally bumping into her will seem like just a coincidence, but not so close that it registers on the dry-hump meter. Some hallways are better suited for copping a feel than others. For example, many college campuses have very wide hallways to suggest a "free flow of ideas" or a similar abstract notion that some narcissistic architect tried to convey with his design in the hopes that he would some day be praised for his underappreciated genius.

Larger hallways may make it difficult for you to find yourself "accidentally" bumping into anyone. Your best bet in this case is to wait until a class gets out so the hallway is full of people. Your odds of scoring a good feel increase with the number of people in the hallway. You may find that the communication or education departments will yield the highest number of females per capita. This is because many hot nineteen-year-old undergrads will gravitate toward degrees that won't challenge them or yield realistic job opportunities, since hot women usually don't need to worry about things like bills and taxes because there are plenty of loaded middle-age doctors and lawyers looking for trophy wives to make up for lost time spent studying.

So you're in the education department surrounded by hot chicks standing around twirling their hair, you've found a tight ass, now what? Just follow these simple steps:

STEP 1:

Carry a stack of things with you. It doesn't matter what you're carrying, just as long as it looks cumbersome to carry. Make sure at least one of the items is a lightweight notebook or a folder.

Drop one of the lighter items behind the subject's feet, by her heels (Figure 4). It's important not to drop anything too heavy because you'll blow your cover and, what's worse, that you will waste calories bending over to pick up your belongings for nothing.

Figure 4: Setting the wheels in motion...

STEP 2:

Get in close to your subject and crouch down behind her. It's important here to bend with your knees, not with your back. You'll see why shortly.

Once in the crouching position, look down at your item and move your head in as close to her ass as possible without actually touching it. Next, reach down with one hand to grab your item, and simultaneously reach up with the other to cop a feel. Immediately after contact, pull your hand away before she has a chance to turn around (Figure 5).

Figure 5: What's that touching her ass? Was it some guy innocently bumping his head as he picked up his belongings, or something more sinister?

If you've done it successfully, it should look like your head bumped into her ass accidentally as you went down to pick up your item—a plausible, if suspicious, event. This will probably creep her out, and rightly so. When she walks away, you're in the clear to congratulate yourself with a quiet "yes!"

Practicing on the ass battlefield is great for beginners, but those with a bit more experience may want to move on to high-value targets that are a bit more challenging. Only after you have mastered the butt-grope will you be prepared to move to the next level. It is said that a coin with risk on one side has reward on the other. This is especially true with the next target.

THE BREAST

A woman's chest is the holy grail of flesh grapplers. No target is more sought-after, and yet, no target is more daunting. The path to chest grabbing is a perilous one that has sent many brazen men crashing down in defeat, humiliation, and occasionally jail time. Copping a feel on a breast is difficult for two reasons: 1. Its location on the body is front and center, below the woman's face, in direct line of sight, and 2. A woman's breast is very sensitive to touch—so much so that women can be induced into orgasm by merely rubbing against them in an elevator; happens all the time.

While it may seem impossible, many men before you have expended a great deal of time and energy conquering this challenge. The result? A handful of techniques, finely crafted and sophisticated. As before, we'll start out with a basic maneuver and move on to more advanced techniques.

A great place to make an initial attempt for the bosom is in a car. It only works if the woman is in the passenger seat and the man is driving.[2] The gist of this approach is to artificially cause the woman to lean forward, using the momentum of your car. This method may seem intuitive at first, but you should exercise careful planning and restraint for successful execution. Here's how:

STEP 1: This step works best in a busy city. If you happen to live in a rural town, move.

While you're driving, look for an opportunity to slam on your brakes. Stale green lights are perfect for the occasion. Try to spot a light that's been green for at least 15 seconds; it's best to do this from the distance of at least one block away.

Now comes the tricky part: divert your passenger's attention to something outside her window, pointing your arm to an object to her right, so that your arm is already in position for the next step (Figure 6).

STEP 2: With your arm in place, all that's left is to bring the car to an abrupt stop to send your unsuspecting subject's tits into your dirty hands. Try to time your stop eight to ten feet away from the intersection.

Figure 6

2. As God intended.

Figure 7: Success! Enjoy it, you manipulative bastard.

If you pull it off, the light should change red just as you get to the stop line, giving you a good excuse to slam on your breaks.

This part requires a great deal of self-discipline because it contradicts man's every instinct to "run the yellow."

Make sure to open your hand at the last second to palm her chest, otherwise your efforts will have gone to waste (Figure 7).

The momentum method can be an especially useful choice if you happen to be good at feigning sincerity. A successful completion will not only give you the satisfaction of touching her boobs but also makes you seem like you were concerned over the well-being of your passenger; it's a win-win. Keep in mind that for this to work, she has to believe that your arm was on her chest to prevent her from suffering the mild abrasions sometimes associated with seatbelt locking. Don't let her suggest that the airbags would have protected her. Bags of air are no substitute for a real man's arm.

While this method is useful, it only gives you a superficial feel of her breast. It barely registers as a touch, let alone a fully realized grope. If you want to go for gold, you need to step up to the next level. You need to maximize your palm-to-tit surface area, and there are only a few ways to do this without getting slapped. Your best bet is to blend in with a crowd, and there's no better place than at a concert.

Concerts are not only great for chest grabbers, but they're also great for the lazy ass-gropers who don't want to put forth the effort and planning it takes to touch an ass in a day-to-day setting. But before you make an attempt, you need to survey your surroundings to scope out the location of all the hot chicks. This can be tricky because women at rock concerts usually don't go up to the very front where they're likely to get their asses kicked, so they tend to stay further back in the crowd. The catch is that the front is usually where you'll find the best prospects for breast grabbing, because the masses tend to pack tight in the front like idiots so they can get closer to the band, because the band members take note of the people up front so they can become friends after the show.

Luckily, not all women are afraid of the crowds up front, and once you've spotted a target, the first thing you need to do is get in position. Here are the specific steps you need to take.

Figure 8: You (1), your scapegoat (2), and your target (3).

STEP 1: The best position to be in for this maneuver is standing behind a guy who's standing behind her (Figure 8). This step is critical, because this guy will be your scapegoat, unless he happens to be her boyfriend, in which case you're on your own. Don't worry about the details too much though, things usually work out.

STEP 2: Weave your arm through the crowd to reach the side of your target; you may need to feel around a bit for her breast. Since space is limited, it will be difficult for her to turn around quickly.

Figure 9: You should have a blank look on your face. Look straight ahead as you get acquainted with her breast. She might suspect the person standing behind her as the culprit, but never the person standing behind him. Never.

Her first inclination will be to look down in disbelief at the hand groping her chest (Figure 9). Don't let this dissuade you. Just because she sees your hand doesn't mean she knows whom it belongs to.

STEP 3: Most concerts are poorly lit, making it difficult for your subject to discern distinguishable facial features, even if she happens to turn around quickly.

This extra cover should give you ample time to pump her breast once, maybe twice, tops (Figure 10). Any more than that, and it means one of two things: she's either into it (which should send you psycho-bitch signals like crazy), or she might not have a pulse. Just don't get carried away.

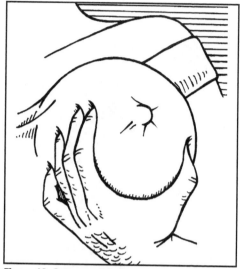

Figure 10: Get a good feel—you're in the safety zone.

As she turns around, release the tit and let your arm fall gently to your side. Since success of this operation depends on your ability to look natural, it's worth emphasizing that you need to be looking straight ahead of you as if nothing has happened. When she finally turns around, do not make eye contact! If you were at a concert and someone standing in front of you suddenly turned around, would you normally make eye contact? Of course not, so don't start being social now. Act natural and play it cool. Pulling this one off will make you a pro, and then it's your duty to give back to collective manhood by teaching future generations how to cop a feel and get away with it.

is for...
TAKING A DUMP

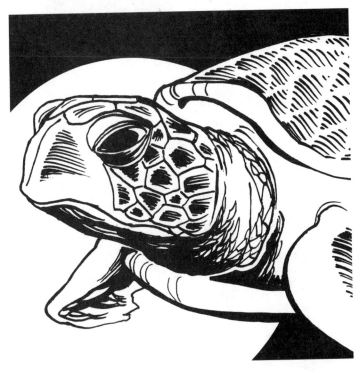

POSSIBLY THE PUREST FORM OF SATISFACTION a man can derive from life is the satisfaction that comes from taking a really good shit. I have, on more than one occasion, called my friends to tell them of my fecal conquests, and likewise, concluded many relationships with these tales.

One of the great things about taking a dump is the solitude you get when you spend a little time on your throne. Most men take three or more dumps per day. Not always out of necessity, but sometimes just to get away from their nagging girlfriends and droning wives. Even the most frigid old hag will temporarily yield her bitching when it comes time for you to make a donation to the children of Crapistan.

The phrase "taking a dump" is a bit of a misnomer because you don't actually take a dump so much as you leave one—and where you leave one is up to you (Figure 1)!

One of the more dignified reasons a man might spend so much time on the shitter is because men are more productive there. Here's a short list of things men do while taking a dump:

• **PHONE CALL TO YOUR MOTHER:** I call my mom all the time from the toilet. Since you have to be there anyway, it's a great way to keep in touch with your family without feeling like you're wasting your time.

Other than the slight echo, she'll be oblivious to your dishonorable discharge. If you're particularly skilled at pulling off the shit-call,

Figure 1

you don't have to limit conversations to relatives and acquaintances. I've closed more than one business deal while doing my business. I won't give details, but let's just say that you might not be reading a certain book about manliness if it weren't for my expert bowel discipline.

The only major pitfall to avoid is noise: fans, dripping, loud shit blasts, and the toilet flush—the most difficult sound to explain. Here are a few explanations for each:

Fan: You have a bad connection/it's windy outside/outright lie (i.e., "I don't hear anything").

Dripping: You're washing your hands/you're washing dishes/outright lie (i.e., "What dripping?").

Loud shit blasts: A car backfired/you dropped a roll of coins into a tub of oatmeal.

Toilet flush: Express indignation that he or she would suggest that you would go to the bathroom during a phone call. If that doesn't work, resort to extreme sarcasm, "Yeah right, I'm taking a shit while I talk on the phone. Oh, that reminds me, hold on a second while I wipe my ass." Then really wipe your ass and come back on the phone and call him an "idiot."

With a bit of practice, creative explanation, or a mute button, the party you're speaking to will be none the wiser to your deuce dropping detour.

•**LEARN CHINESE:** Mandarin is a difficult language to learn, but a useful one if you ever plan on traveling to China or the engineering department at a university. Unless you spend several hours per day practicing, you'll find yourself in a Chinese restaurant munching on a bowl of bull testicles because of your crippling illiteracy.

•**EAT:** Eating on the shitter is a monument to efficiency. Feeding the shit-sharks is a tiring task that requires a great deal of energy; why wait until you're off the pot to replenish that lost energy later on in the day when you might risk dying of fatigue? In fact, when you consider what's at stake, you can't afford not to eat on the throne.

I once knew this guy who used to take his food into the bathroom every day during lunch until one day his manager caught him. When pressed for an explanation, he told his boss about his efficiency theory, and his boss was so impressed that he let him take a permanent vacation to write a book about manliness.

SURVIVAL TIPS

FRIEND'S HOUSE: The worst-case scenario when using a bathroom at a friend's house is realizing that there's no toilet paper after you've backed one out. The reason this is such a dreadful scenario is because you're completely at the mercy of your friend, and he, by the male code of spite, is obliged to be as big of a dick as possible. For example, he might:

- Not care
- Open the door and mock you for your vulnerability
- Having opened the door, invite everyone over for a party
- Make you wipe with tampons

Fortunately, there are a few options at your disposal, so you won't have to rely on his dubious empathy. The first is to use the shower curtains. While not ideal, shower curtains provide enough surface area to get the job done. The down side is that shower curtains are made out of vinyl—which tends to make sharp edges when creased—so you might as well be wiping your ass with sheet metal. Another option is to use the floor mat, but its shag carpeting may prove to be too lumpy and cumbersome. Also, your friend probably walks all over it barefoot when he gets out of the shower, and you don't want that funk anywhere near your corn hole. Your best bet would be to use his hand towels. For an added bonus, you could neatly fold them and put them back in his linen closet for a surprise. Make sure to wash your hands with those fancy seashell-shaped display soaps he has on the counter, then stop being his friend for having them.

WILDERNESS: Being caught in the wilderness without toilet paper isn't as bad as you might think. After your initial panic has subsided, a moment of observation will yield a surplus of ass-wiping fodder at the ready. While there is the typical fare of material such as pinecones and twigs for the hardasses, there's an often-overlooked resource that people don't immediately think of: wildlife. Take a squirrel, for example. Squirrels are soft, everywhere, and they love nuts.

THE DUMP DICTIONARY

Now we know a lot about the different things to do while taking a dump and what to do in emergency situations, but what about the different kinds of dumps we can take? Here's a brief primer.

THE IMPOSSIBLE FIRE HOSE: This is one of those shits you take where everything comes out in one smooth motion and only requires one cut; the result often resembles a fire hose or resting python. These are exceedingly rare occurrences, which is why they're referred to as "impossible."

THE EVENT HORIZON: When you lay so much brick that the output forms a small hill that rises above the surface of the water in the bowl. Low-fill toilets don't count. Courtesy flush encouraged.

CHOCOLATE SHOTGUN: This is what happens when explosive diarrhea meets a weak O-ring.

RING OF FIRE: A common occurrence when you drink the water in developing countries resulting in dysentery. After the third or fourth day, there will be literally nothing in your bowels to shit out, so the only thing left is stomach acid.

GREAT BALLS OF FIRE: When you have the above and you wipe from back to front.

THE "I MOVED TO HOLLYWOOD": When you spend a lot of time and energy in preparation, try really hard, and nothing comes out.

CASPER THE FRIENDLY COMPOST: When you've had nothing but piña coladas to eat or drink for twenty-four hours straight, your yield will literally become white. Try it!

THE GIRLFRIEND: Keeps going, and going, and going . . .

THE SURVIVOR: When you think you're done and you wipe, a solitary turd pushes through at the last minute. This is usually the cause of clogged toilets because many people forget to flush after they wipe the first time. The second unit of toilet paper overwhelms most toilets, and you end up having to mop shit off the floor. Or if you're a guest at someone's house, sprint to your car.

THE PRISON BREAK: When you're pucker-butting for over thirty minutes, and you have to go up a flight of stairs, the stimulation will give way to a turtle head that will exploit a crack in the wall, letting one loose in your trousers and making you the butt of jokes for years to come.

 is for...
ENLIGHTENMENT

A. Vildasol

QUICKLY, NAME TWO FAMOUS WOMEN INVENTORS.
Too hard? Okay, name one. How about a famous invention
made by a woman? Give up? That's because there are none.
Men invented everything. From Plato's momentous discovery of wrestling

(Figure 1), to John Holmes's perfection of the money shot, all notable milestones of human achievement have come about because of men.

Modern researchers have made estimates regarding the earliest known evidence of the discovery of fire, but they maintain that nobody knows the exact date of this celebrated first encounter. But c'mon, we all know when fire was really discovered. It was found the second that man realized that animals were made out of meat. Since Eve's

Figure 1: Plato often contemplated the question of whether one could be taught virtue. He regularly invoked the flying elbow as a pedagogical method in which the master conveys his elbow to the pupil's skull repeatedly, and through this repetition, the pupil eventually comes to enlightenment. Or a coma.

better half, Adam, was the first man on Earth, he was the discoverer of fire. Problem solved, question answered.

Speaking of Adam, it's worth mentioning some of the other noteworthy nuggets of enlightenment he came across before that bitch Eve stuffed her face full of fruit from the tree of knowledge, robbing man of eternal life.

ADAM—THE PIONEER OF SLACKING

In the beginning, when God created the heavens—a vast and expansive cloud of dust and gas that eventually coalesced into planets revolving around a hydrogenous fusion core—he also fancied creating Earth, a planet ripe with the dust of creation. Being the resourceful God that he is, he decided to put all this dust to good use and to create man from it. It took millions of years and countless particles of matter to culminate in the creation of man, and what does Adam do when he's put on Earth? What every red-blooded man does when he gets some free time: nothing (Figure 2). In his early years, Adam spent most of his time loafing around, limp-wristed out of contempt for all the hard-working animals around him. The ancient Greek statesman Aesop once told a fable about the ant and the grasshopper, in which the diligent ants labored tirelessly throughout the spring and summer months to store food for the winter, while the grasshopper laughed and played, mocking his arthropodic brethren for working so hard.

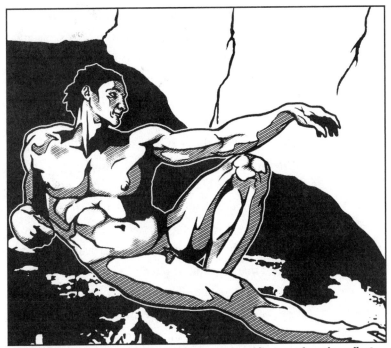

Figure 2: Adam, seen here bored off his ass, undertaking one of man's earliest endeavors: loafing.

Adam, like the grasshopper, disdains those nimble, overly productive creatures that give the rest of us a bad name. When winter came, the grasshopper met his cold and bitter demise as he starved while watching the ants reap the fruits of their labor. Adam, unlike the grasshopper, did not starve when winter came because man was endowed with resourcefulness and cunning. So he did what every man does when he gets hungry: he made his woman cook. This bold experiment in laziness paved the path for the men who came after Adam, which is all of them.

ADAM—HOW BLAME BECAME

Adam was one of the most prolific innovators of his time, but simply stating so doesn't do justice to his brand of lackadaisical genius since there were few others vying for the title in his era. One other, to be exact. But historians don't prescribe much value to Eve's nagging toward the contribution of humanity's intellect. Along with destroying our bid for immortality, Eve set the ball in motion for feminine inadequacy for millennia to come.

That leads us to her infamous deed: eating the fruit from the tree of knowledge. Here's a question that not a lot of people think about: What if the culprit was really Adam? Not possible? Think about it; what could be more spiteful than breaking the only law (which is really the same as breaking every law), then bailing out and letting an entire gender take the heat for it? It's too tempting not to consider. Here's how it could have played out: maybe Adam was feeling particularly hungry that day, and he decided that it would be bitchin' if he could grab a bite to eat and disobey a divine mandate all on his lunch break. Or maybe he wanted to eat the apple just to see if he could get away with it unscathed, much like a child standing up on a roller coaster ride at an amusement park in spite of all the warnings. Whatever the reason, it's possible that Adam was the one who ate the forbidden fruit. After all, history would later prove that men are almost supernaturally wise.

After doing the misdeed, Adam might have put his newfound knowledge to good use by passing the buck on to Eve when God came asking (Figure 3). The conversation might have gone something like this:

Figure 3: Dodging the wrath.

GOD: Who hath grazed from the tree of knowledge?

ADAM: Someone ate from the tree?

GOD: The tree of knowledge.

ADAM: Yeah, wow. Uh . . . that's just . . . wow. I don't know what to say.

GOD: Do you know anything about it?

ADAM: Well, I did notice something the other day, but . . .

GOD: But what?

ADAM: Never mind. I shouldn't have said anything; you probably wouldn't be interested anyway.

GOD: C'mon, tell me! You have to tell me, you can't do that!

ADAM: Do what?

GOD: Say you know a secret and not tell me! Just give me a hint.

ADAM: Well, okay. Now, I'm not saying Eve ate the apple, but let's just say that she's been talking to Satan a lot lately.

GOD: Get out!

ADAM: Yep. They've been talking about lots of things. Temptation, bearing false witness, possibly fruit. Oops, here she comes.

EVE: Hey, guys.

ADAM: Hey, Eve. So did you hear about the tree of knowledge?

EVE: No, what about it?

ADAM: Someone ate from the tree.

EVE: What? That's terrible. Any idea who did it?

ADAM: No idea, do you know anything?

EVE: This is the first time I've heard about it.

GOD: Don't make this difficult. I know you've been talking to Satan.

EVE: I don't know what you're talking about. Who told you that?

GOD: I have my sources.

EVE: I swear to—you—that I didn't eat the apple!

ADAM: Listen, God, I have a confession to make: I ate the apple.

GOD: That's very nice of you, Adam, but you don't have to defend her. You've been a great help already.

EVE: Adam, what did you tell him?

ADAM: I don't want to get involved. This is between you two.

GOD: Just come clean and we can move on.

EVE: It wasn't me!

GOD: Then who?

EVE: I don't know! Jesus!

GOD: Oh, c'mon now, he hasn't even been born yet, that's the best you can come up with?

EVE: No, not Jesus the proper noun, I meant like "Jesus!" the exclamation.

GOD: Now you're being facetious. I'm tired of playing these games. Since you won't fess up, I have no choice but to damn your gender.

EVE: But—

GOD: Damned.

EVE: Adam, tell him!

ADAM: I'd like to help you out, Eve, honest, but my hands are tied on this.

GOD: You can start by making seventy-five cents for every dollar a man makes.

And that's how Eve fucked it up for the entire female gender, thanks in part to Adam's clever pioneering of the instrument of blame. As abundant as Adam's innovations were, there were other notable men who tread the path of enlightenment after him.

ODIN—THE PATRON SAINT OF REARRANGING YOUR FACE

Odin is the manliest of all mythological gods. Nobody even comes close to Odin. Thor? Please. Zeus? Get the fuck out of my office. Zeus was possibly the biggest pussy in all of mythology. His specialty was to roll over and take it in the corn hole. Lesser gods such as Ares, Poseidon, and his bitch wife, Hera, were always pushing Zeus around and walking all over him. The only thing Zeus ever did was turn people into rocks or mountains, and he could hurl an occasional lightning bolt. Ooo, a lightning bolt! Oh no, not that, anything but a lightning bolt! Look out, Zeus the all powerful will smite you just as long as you aren't standing next to a long pole.

Unlike Zeus, Odin was a god who could get things done. Odin didn't fuck around with lightning bolts, he took care of assailants by smothering them with his giant nuts. Odin was the Norse god of war, wisdom, magic, victory, hunting, and poetry. Yes, poetry. Although poetry is pretty much the unmanliest form of writing, Odin was man enough to make even this most effeminate of written forms rock tits. Here's a haiku written by Odin:

> *I murdered a man.*
> *He had a wife and two kids.*
> *I slept peacefully.*

Here's a poem Odin wrote one day when he ordered a sandwich, and they were out of wheat (Odin eats a diet high in fiber because cholesterol kills):

> *Bitch, say what?*

That's all he wrote before he stomped his foot up her ass and wore her colon around his ankle.

If there was one word to describe Odin, it would be cocksure. Odin had no character flaws, unless you consider an excessively violent response to minor annoyances a character flaw, and I don't. Case in point: One time some guy went to one of Odin's temples to sacrifice himself in an effort to spare his village from the famine that was scientifically proven to be caused by Odin.

The guy tried to impale himself on a large stake, but he lost his balance and fell awkwardly on the pole, causing him to bleed all over the place. When Odin came down to collect the man's soul, he saw the mess and became furious because Odin hates a sloppy sacrifice. Odin was so pissed that he resurrected the man, ate him, and then poked his own eye out and ate it so he could watch the body as he digested it and shit it out.

SOCRATES—THE FATHER OF SPITE

My advice to you is to get married: if you find a good wife, you'll be happy; if you get a bad one, you'll become a philosopher.—**Socrates**

Socrates was a philosopher. He was married to an irritable old crone, Xanthippe, whose nagging was legendary. Xanthippe had modest cognitive ability, and it's rumored that the reason Socrates was so proficient at demolishing asses during debates is because of the sheer level of stupidity he had to deal with daily. Socrates often said that Xanthippe was the most difficult person to live with, because after having dealt with her brand of bullshit, he asserted that he could easily get along with anyone else.

Xanthippe was notoriously thickheaded. The smartest thing to ever come out of Xanthippe's mouth was Socrates's cock. Socrates eagerly had three children with Xanthippe, not because he wanted children, but because he wanted to put her through the pain of childbirth three times. He would have had a fourth child if he weren't seriously concerned that his penis would fall off due to frostbite (Figure 4).

Figure 4: Xanthippe's vagina.

is for...
FEMALE WRESTLING

THERE'S ONLY ONE THING in this universe hotter than females wrestling, and that's females wrestling in hot oil.[1] Naked. There's something about chicks wrestling that brings people of the world together across ethnic and national boundaries, allowing us to put aside our differences and enjoy a spectacle together that touches us all on a profound—and largely physiological—level.

1. Wrestling in cold oil would be stupid. And just when you thought I was using superfluous adjectives . . .

What sharply distinguishes female wrestling from its male counterpart is that when guys fight, their cocks never flop out (Figure 1), they don't end up naked on the floor, and they don't accidentally make out. As opposed to women, who, by necessity, always end up naked and usually make out. If there's a possibility of their breasts flying out, they will fly out. Don't mistake the grunts of combat as the venting of hostility: they're moans of longing.

Figure 1: Never happens.

FEMALE WRESTLING

The allure of female wrestling comes from the possibility of an erotic event between two or more competitors (don't discount tag team female wrestling) occurring during the match. This is known as the lesbian probability.

> *Theorem: There exists a function P defined for an erotic lesbian encounter E such that the probability of a given encounter $1 \geq P(E) \geq 0$. That is, lesbian probability reflects how likely it is for a particular erotic event to occur.*

With every match-up comes the possibility of any number of erotic events to occur. Due to the full contact nature of wrestling, it's inevitable for the contenders to have a sexually suggestive encounter.

Here's a short list of what to look for, and the lesbian probability of each event (E).

E = Tit rub: Like its name suggests, the tit rub is what happens when the wrestlers lock arms while attempting to topple each other; the close proximity of their chests makes it likely for the contenders' breasts to rub against each other. The more aggressive the contenders, the sloppier the tit rub becomes. Naturally, larger breasts are more conducive to this event.

Figure 2: Shimmy to the left, shimmy to the right . . .

There are two basic types of tit rubbing to look out for: the tit shimmy, a side-to-side tit rubbing that occurs when one or both wrestlers move their chests horizontally during contact (Figure 2), and the tit swirl, a circular rubbing motion (Figure 3).

Tit rubbing is a very common occurrence during female wrestling matches. Let's just say that if you traded chest friction as a commodity, you'd get invited to ring the opening bell at the New York Stock Exchange.

P(Tit Rub) = 80%

E = Wardrobe Malfunction: This is by far the most boner-inducing event to happen during a match. The wardrobe malfunction takes

Figure 3: The titty swirl, sometimes referred to as the milk shake.

place during an intense wrestling bout when one of the contenders "accidentally" rips the bikini strap or pulls the thong string of the other competitor. Not to be outdone, the partially unclothed contender will feel angry and humiliated, so she will retaliate with an equivalent malfunction. If the initial unclothing was an actual accident, this will infuriate the initiator, causing her to strike back since she originally unclothed her competitor by mistake, as opposed to her competitor who did it out of malice. Within seconds of the first unveiling, both wrestlers will be completely naked. Any reputable referee will call the match at this point, but in practice, the referee knows better than to get involved, lest his ass get whopped by the crowd.

P(WARDROBE MALFUNCTION) = 20%

FEMALE WRESTLING

E = TIT PUNCH: In principle, closed-fisted attacks are forbidden because women have glass jaws. That said, referees look the other way when a tit punch occurs, due to the likelihood of a grope to follow.

P(TIT PUNCH) = 40%

E = BREAST GROPE: A breast grope is a tit punch gone wrong in the rightest way possible. Since the likelihood of this outcome is conditional, a simple application of Baye's theorem will help us relate the probabilities of these events:

Figure 4: Bam! Right in the cakehole.

P(BREAST GROPE | TIT PUNCH) = 10%

E = CROTCH KICK: When I hear the word "sexy," the first thing that comes to mind is a woman getting kicked in the baby maker (Figure 4). Female wrestlers have hymens made of steel, and nothing short of a frank chop to the clams will register on the sexometer. This is one of the more advanced stages of eroticism in the ring, and unfortunately it's a relatively rare occurrence.

P(CROTCH KICK) = 1%

THE FUTURE OF FEMALE WRESTLING

Although wrestling originated as a way for two men to settle disputes, over the years women have proven themselves worthy of stepping into the ring. Nobody knows for sure what the future holds for female wrestling, except for me. As technological progress continues, robots that are also lesbians will replace women (Figure 5).

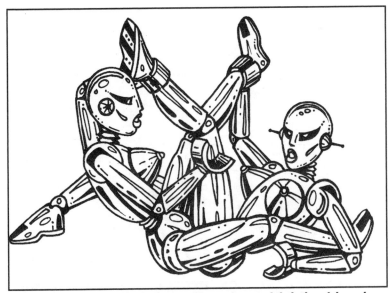

Figure 5: Lesbian robots in the future will spend most of their time doing scissors and shooting lasers out of their eyes.

 is for... **GAS**

THERE'S A REASON PEOPLE USE THE PHRASE "timeless humor" when referring to the act of passing gas. That's because farts are always funny. Always. There's nothing in the world that's funnier than the sound of gas forced through the anus in discrete pockets of air that cause your buttocks to flap with a charming rhythm. Fart jokes are unique from all other jokes in that the delivery is the punch line and the punch line is the delivery. There's no setup, no call back, and no awkward malapropisms with fart jokes, just a fart giver (farter) and a fart taker (fartee).

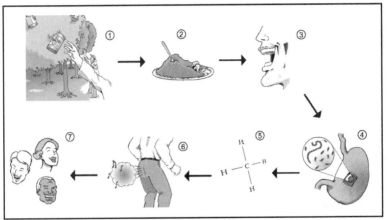

Figure 1: Sun-ripened beans are harvested from bean trees (1), processed for consumption and served for dinner alongside other flatulence-inducing foods such as broccoli (2). The meal is then scarfed down, causing excess air to be swallowed along with every bite (3). The food travels down your esophagus to your stomach, where your body's natural bacteria and yeasts break down the food (4), helping digest your meal and giving off methane as a byproduct (5). Once the methane is inside you, the molecules collect in your colon, where your sphincter finally releases the pressure—usually due to exhaustion or malice— producing a jovial noise in the process (6). The ensuing sound will be heard by colleagues, who will laugh heartily and express their admiration of your procto- logical proclamation (7).

The actual farter-fartee system is a bit more complex than that and deserves a closer inspection (Figure 1).

It's worth noting in this process that the sound made depends on several factors, such as moisture, pressure, strength of your sphincter, and the density of the air that is expelled from your rectum. Here's a brief explanation of each of these factors and how they relate to deliv- ering a satisfying fart:

• **MOISTURE:** Next to pressure, the wetness of a fart plays the biggest role in the delivery of a robust, seat-rattling roar. A wet fart on a hard wooden bench during a sermon can make the difference between a fart that gets a few chuckles and stink eyes from stuck-up church hags, and a legendary fart that people will refer to with statements like "remember that one time that guy got kicked out of church for busting ass?" What makes a wet fart especially endearing is the subtle imagery it invokes. Who among us hasn't been thrilled by the dampened noise of bubbles popping as they ooze up through thick mud? Letting off a juicy one conjures up similar images of air bubbles laboring through a viscous ass substance to make an amusing flapping noise (Figure 2).

There are a number of causes of moist farts. A few of the more common reasons are: crack sweat, an especially flabby butt, a failure to wipe thoroughly, or a diet rich in glutinous substances. Sometimes a fart can start out dry, but end up wet. Of these reasons, only the latter won't get you socially ostracized, though having to wipe afterward won't score you any points with the ladies. Sometimes a wet fart is known as a "juicy dialectic"; that is to say, it's a constant strug-

Figure 2: There's no shame in having to wipe after an especially loud wet fart.

gle between nasty and awesome. Exercise caution when you decide it's time for a wet one.

• **PRESSURE:** There's an old adage that states the reason women can't fart loud is because women don't keep their mouths shut long enough to build pressure. While this explanation is consistent with everything we know about the science of farting, the amount of pressure a fart can have also depends on fart frequency. It's quite simple: fart too much, and your farts will be short and weak. Fart less frequently and your farts will be powerful and awe-inspiring. Under no circumstance should you force out a fart; if you don't feel the pressure built up inside you, save it. A fart should come to you naturally, like a spring blossom.

Forcing a fart prematurely will result in a weak, high-pitched sound that tapers off quickly and anticlimactically. Not only will your forced flatulence be aurally impotent but these underdeveloped farts can also cause embarrassing spillage. A person who forces a poor fart for the sake of a laugh is called a "faker" (Figure 3).

The reason pressure is so important to a fart is because the velocity of a fart is proportional to the pressure built up inside the colon. A greater fart velocity means a greater frequency of "fart ripples," or "fripples."

A fripple is the unit of measurement of a fart starting from silence, to sound, then back to silence again.

Figure 3: Nobody likes a faker.

For example, the shortest sound that can be considered a fart is 1 fripple.[1] Healthy farts normally have dozens of fripples because of the built-up pressure giving each fart wave an elongated period, but forced farts have few—usually indiscernible—fripples resulting from a lack of pressure (Figure 4).

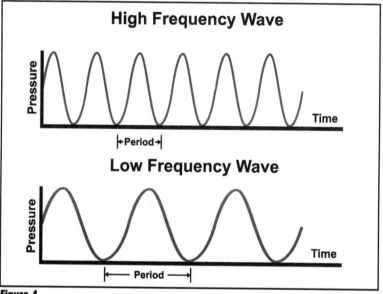

Figure 4

• **SPHINCTERAL STRENGTH:** Not only critical for making a clean cut while taking a dump, the strength of your sphincter is an often-overlooked component of farting. If you have a weak muscle, you won't be able to keep your butt hole shut tight enough to build pressure. Instead, you'll find yourself "leaking" all the time. This is a highly undesirable condition that causes you to constantly stink,

1. This is usually a short "brrraap" sound, which if repeated in succession, will produce the sound commonly known as a fart.

wafting your odors behind you like a kite tail wherever you go. Sometimes you may want to leave a trail of your stink behind, but not if you can't control it (more on this later).

If you happen to have a weak o-ring, are you doomed to smell like shit the rest of your life, or is there something that can be done about it? Fortunately, there are a few things you can do to improve your sphincteral health:

1) Stop taking it up the ass. If you're prone to kinky sex like fisting or strange object insertion, cut it out. Your ass is not a storage space. If you find yourself sticking things up your ass when you're bored, what you need is a hobby. Consider fishing or collecting bottle caps, but don't put the fish or the bottle caps up your ass.

2) Shave. While it's manly to have a beard, having too much beard will make you look like a drifter, or worse, a hippy. This can cause problems when you're trying to get through airport security. Shaving will help improve the health of your anus by reducing the likelihood of a cavity search.

3) Cut down on cheese and foods heavy in oils. Too much oil will make it difficult to keep your shit-tube shut when you want to build pressure, and too much cheese will make it difficult to open.

• **DENSITY:** A fart's density is usually an indicator of a fart's potency. Once free from the confines of your colon, a fart will briefly rise, and then as it cools, it will begin to descend on its surroundings like a thick blanket of fog, asphyxiating animals and small children

Figure 5: Skip the ambulance; it's already too late.

around it (Figure 5). The best kinds of farts are the ones you can feel—not just indirectly through vibrations, but the actual weight of the fart itself. Some farts are so thick, so massive, that they can manipulate, and be manipulated by, solid objects around you.

When someone drops a shit bomb next to you, you need to act fast to shovel that ass-bouquet away from you as quickly as possible, lest your olfactory nerves pay the ultimate price. Grab something and start fanning it away from you, toward the direction of the assailant if you can. Though it's not possible to get 100 percent of the offending scent away from you, you can usually get up to 70 percent of the blast deflected if you get it early enough.

SPREADING THE WEALTH

A fart that isn't smelt is a fart surely wasted. What good is it to let one off if you can't share your fecal phantom with your friends and co-workers? Even worse, if people never farted, all the gasses released from farting—nitrogen, oxygen and methane—would eventually disappear, causing the slow and eventual suffocation of the entire planet. Farting is the only type of recycling a man should take part in.

Though farts can be deflected and evaded, there are some techniques that can aid you in administering a dose of your personal funk more effectively.

One way to make your fart leave a lasting impression is to make it more potent than it would normally be. You can do this by focusing it with the special "hadoken" technique (Figures 6–7, on the next page).

If you prefer a less direct approach, you can opt to deploy a number of stealth techniques to evacuate your shit shoot. Covert flatulence will give you a great opportunity to not only make others experience your most unsavory of scents, but it will also give you a chance to point your finger to make your innocent colleagues take the blame (if it happens to be an especially bad one).

THE ESCALATOR

Crowded escalators are the perfect place to drop a bomb because it's nearly impossible to tell who the perpetrator is. The best location on an escalator to let loose is near the bottom third of the stretch, as opposed to when you first get on. The reason you should wait a bit is to check to make sure that other patrons will get behind you, otherwise it's a wasted

GAS

Figure 6: Immediately after farting, use your hands to collect and compact your atmospheric discharge, like you would if you were making a snowball. Make sure to put your palms next to your hip to get the most leverage for the next step.

Figure 7: With your anal aura packed tightly in your hands, swing your hands out in front of your chest, putting your palms together, facing outward toward your opponent. Make sure to yell "hadoken!" as you do this to startle your opponent. If done correctly, your victim should become overwhelmed by your ass blast, and will attempt to hold back tears from his or her watering eyes.

effort. Try to fluctuate the sphincteral muscle so that your fart makes only the slightest audible footprint—nothing more than the slightest hiss—then sit back and enjoy as the people behind you slowly traverse through your shit trail (see Figure 8, opposite). This is one of the few occasions where having a loose colon might be slightly advantageous.

VENTS

Another great way to disperse your stench without getting noticed is by farting in front of an air conditioner, a fan, or an air intake vent. Of these places, a fan is probably your best bet for a clean execution because an air conditioner that's set too high might cool your fart down very fast, causing it to sink to the floor before it hits anyone's nostrils, while most air intake vents are so large that your farts will be

Figure 8: Pay close attention to the response of others on the escalator and try to mimic their reactions so as to give the illusion that someone ahead of you is the culprit. If you're riding with a friend, you could even go so far as to say something like "oh man, do you smell that?" Just remember to speak in a low voice and try not to seem too obvious. This will make you seem reserved and considerate of others' feelings. Give the perception that you're sensitive of people who might have hygienic deficiencies—not that you give a shit about offending some stank-ass—but remember, your goal here is stealth, not spite.

diluted in the catacombs of insulation. The stealth aspect of cutting one in front of a fan comes from the amorphous nature of a gas cloud, making it difficult to trace the origin of a gas passer with any degree of accuracy. This is your chance to pawn off your misdeed on someone else, but not before you build a sizeable repertoire of blame and counterblame strategies.

DODGING THE BULLET

Shifting the blame of a fart from you to someone else doesn't require much effort if you come prepared. Don't be lulled into a false sense of security just because you've gotten away with it in the past; you always need to bring your A-game to the table. As mentioned earlier, one way to shift the blame is to ask questions—that is, put on your best poker face, play dumb, and pretend you don't know what happened. While this approach works, it's a bit passive and has a degree of uncertainty involved, like a game of Russian roulette. For example, if you're in a room of five people, you know for a fact that someone farted because you can all smell it. Someone will eventually take the blame, so although pretending like it wasn't you can be useful, it's not a foolproof method. Unless you happen to be in a car and passing a refinery, it's impossible to get away with it completely unscathed 100 percent of the time.

This is where the fart-rhyme comes in. It's understood that in all fart disputes, the person who is able to say the cleverest rhyming rebuttal is the innocent party and shall be absolved of all guilt associated with the misdeed, even if he actually did the crime. When two people are well versed in the art of the fart-rhyme the most interesting exchanges take place. For example, here's a hypothetical altercation that serves to demonstrate the potential if two masters battled each other:

GUY 1: Who farted?

GUY 2: He who observed it served it.

GUY 1: He who said the rhyme did the crime.

GUY 2: Whoever spoke last set off the blast.

GUY 1: The next person who speaks is the person who reeks.

GUY 2: The guy who spoke let off the smoke.

GUY 1: The guy with the excuse set the fuse.

GUY 2: He who first detected it ejected it.

GUY 1: . . . I didn't fart.

From this brief exchange, it's clear that Guy 1 is the guilty party because he failed to give a rebuttal in the form of a rhyme. Learn the rhymes and use them; the system never fails.

CLASSIFICATIONS

Though it's good to know how to deflect a fart, it's also important to know how to classify one so that you know how to deal with it. For example, you wouldn't want to try to deflect a fart with couch cushions and pillows if the fart is diffuse. Here is an abridged glossary of gas to help you enrich your ass vocabulary:

BREAKING THE WIND: A classic—almost formal—expression used to refer to the act of passing gas. You can't fix wind that is broken, but since it's abundant on earth, nobody really cares if you break it.

TROPICAL WIND: Like breaking the wind, a tropical wind is gas that comes from the butt of tropical islanders who primarily forage on pineapples, papaya, and coconuts. This gives their flatulence a pleasant, slightly fruity smell, and it's probably good for your skin, too.

THE SECRET RECIPE: A fart comprising eleven secret herbs and spices, usually administered after a dose of chicken. You'd swear you were smelling ½ tsp black pepper, ½ tsp salt, 1 tbsp chopped parsley, 1 tsp MSG, 2 tsp onion powder, ½ tsp paprika, ½ tsp bell seasoning, ½ tsp garlic powder (unsalted), 1 tsp celery powder, ½ tsp seasoned salt, and 1 cup of flour. But you're not. It's a secret.

I CAN'T BELIEVE IT'S NOT BUTTER: Sometimes when a person tries too hard to squeeze one out—perhaps to impress a date or a new friend—he'll squeeze so violently that the fart starts out with a high-pitched squeal that will turn into a low rumbling gurgle. Everyone suspects the worst, but when you go to the bathroom for a safety wipe, you find that you're dry and all is well. In spite of the sound and feeling of slippage, you can't believe that you got lucky enough to avoid the mild shit dribble of a failed fart attempt, sometimes known as butter.

RESIDENT EVIL: Occasionally, a fart will be so bad that no amount of fanning, deodorizers and tears will make it go away. The fart will cake itself in your clothes, carpet, and hair. New cars will never smell the same, and if ground zero happens to be your couch, you'll get a new blast of ass air every time you compress the cushions by sitting on them. These farts can sometimes be so pungent that you can taste them.

A FART FROM THE HEART: When you're in a "romantic" setting with a woman, you look her in the eyes and say "there's something I've been meaning to tell you" then just as her eyes start to water, hold her hands and let one loose. She'll be so pissed that she'll try to slap you, but you're already holding her hands, so hold them tight so she gets a good whiff.

DUTCH OVEN: If you happen to be in bed sleeping with someone, what you do is drop the nastiest, juiciest broccoli fart under the covers. Then, while your partner is still sleeping, lift the covers over her head and then wait until the fart dissipates (Figure 9).

DUTCH OVEN SURPRISE: Like the Dutch oven, but if you force it too hard, you get a surprise batch of freshly baked dutch oven brownies. If it's your bed, get up and change immediately so it doesn't spill. If it's her bed, it can wait until morning.

THE THROAT QUENCHER: This is administered while you're hanging out with a bunch of friends. When one of them passes out on your couch, quietly bring your ass as close to his mouth as possible, then bust that breeze straight down his throat. This dosage may give him strep throat, and may cause permanent scarring.

Figure 9: Gently cover her head. If she wakes up, try to keep her head under the covers for at least ten seconds. The struggling will cause her to take deep breaths, sucking in more of your noxious gas with every desperate gasp for fresh air.

is for...
HOT SAUCE

ALL MEN LOVE SPICY FOOD. The statement "I don't like spicy food" is a more verbose way of saying "I have a vagina." I can't emphasize enough that only pussies don't like spicy food. If you're not convinced, let the facts speak for themselves. The following is a complete list of people who can't handle spicy foods:

- Pregnant women
- Breastfeeding mothers
- Menstruating women
- Women on menopause

- Children
- Old people
- Animals (except for fish[1])

It's worth emphasizing that this is a *complete* list of people who don't like spicy foods, so if you don't like spicy food, then you must be one of the above listed. Animals, old people, and children can't read, so I guess that makes you a bitch.

Pregnant mothers are notorious enemies of hot sauce because they're discouraged from eating spicy foods to protect their unborn children. Aww boo hoo! The poor fetus can't handle a little heat. If I ever made the mistake of having a child, I'd make sure my woman would eat extra spicy food. Any child who can't handle the heat is no child of mine. It's a great way to weed out the pussies before they have a chance to grow up and disappoint us by becoming nine-to-five paper-pushing, ass-kissing, yes-men. If I had things my way, hot sauce would be the ~~primary~~ only ingredient in baby formula.

For fans of spicy food, that is, hairy chested men, it's sometimes difficult to find food with any heat at restaurants. The reason is because people who think they like spicy food go to restaurants, order their food spicy, and then complain when they can't handle it. This has caused a gradual shift toward less spicy recipes in the restaurant industry. Here's a quick guide you can use to determine how spicy your food will be when you order it in a restaurant:

How spicy you order it:	How spicy you get it:
Mild ⟶	Mild
Medium ⟶	Mild
Hot ⟶	Mild
Very Hot ⟶	Mild

---

1. I fed my neighbor's fish hot sauce one time and it loved the spice so much, it started doing tricks like swimming sideways.

HOT SAUCE

COPING WITH HATERS

I lost my best friend when I was eight. Everyone always says, "It can't happen to me," until you wake up one day and everything changes. We were outside burning insects with a magnifying glass when his grandma called us in for lunch. She gave us two choices: hotdogs or spicy sausages. I pushed his grandma aside so I could grab the first spicy sausage, expecting my friend to fight me for it. To my surprise, he was standing in line behind his five sisters waiting for a hotdog. I asked him why he didn't want a spicy sausage, and he said that he didn't like spicy food. I finished my lunch, played some video games, and went home, never to talk to him again—but not before I smashed his glasses.

It was a difficult time for both of us, because I didn't have any other friends who had a Sega Master System, and he didn't have another pair of reading glasses, but I learned something that day: You don't have to lose your friends if they don't like spicy food. At least not always. It's not easy, but it's possible to convert hot-sauce heretics and bring them back to the dark side.

I once had a co-worker who said she didn't like spicy food, so she would always order some bland alfredo dish, then get up to wash her hands after she placed her order. One day when she got up to go to the restroom, her food came, and I decided to put some hot sauce on her plate to make a believer out of her. When she finally returned, I watched anxiously as she chewed her first bite. In the middle of chewing, she clasped her throat and looked up at me with tears in her eyes. Her face became bright red, and she tried to thank me, but she couldn't say the words: "Did you . . . did . . . did . . . you put . . . hot s— . . . I can't eat. . . ." I cut her off and told her she didn't have to thank me. Her tears were enough. She enjoyed the hot sauce so much that her face became itchy and full of satisfaction. Her nose started running and I couldn't tell for sure, but I think her nipples were becoming hard, which only turned me on more. She was gasping for air, sweating bullets, and moaning, so I finally put it all together: she was having an orgasm! Some guy sitting at the table next to me took notice. He got up, wrapped his arms around her stomach, and started thrusting. I wasn't going to let that son of a bitch put the moves on her, so I sucker punched him right in the nose. He went down like Monica, and all the excitement made my co-worker pass out.

She didn't come back to work the next day, or ever again. I think she got a transfer. One caveat with this method is that not every attempt will be successful like this story.

THE BABY

My next door neighbor is a bitch. She has a stupid son who keeps coming back home no matter how many times I jump out of the bushes and scare him, and she keeps feeding him veggie burgers. I've never seen her wear shoes, and I'm not even sure she owns a pair. She has a Jerry Garcia poster in her bedroom, so like I said, a bitch. When I found out that she was pregnant with another child, I wasn't going to let another one of her sons go to waste, so I decided to do her a favor by putting some hair on the kid's chest

After she gave birth, she brought her new son over to show off one day, and that's when I offered to hold him. She was delighted that I had apparently warmed up to kids, so she handed me her son, still feeding on his bottle. When she wasn't looking, I popped open his bottle cap and filled it full of chorizo. The baby seemed like he was loving it at first, but suddenly he started crying, so I did what I always do when babies cry: I put him in the garbage can. His mom started yelling and screaming, then she tried to punch me, so I stepped to the side and she accidentally tripped and fell down four flights of stairs, and then she accidentally got peed on.

I don't want to place too much importance on hot sauce, but I don't think I'm overstepping my bounds when I say hot sauce is to food what salvation is to humanity. Bland people like bland food, and the merit of your character will ultimately be determined by your preference for spicy foods.

is for...

IRATE

IRATE: MAN'S DEFAULT—AND ONLY—EMOTION. Men are always irate; sometimes for good reason, and sometimes for no reason at all. Not to be confused with moody, which is what women become at least once per month, any time you want to take a leak off a bridge (see Figure 1, next page), or any time you want to have sex, which happens to be 100 percent of the time. So in other words, being moody is a woman's natural response to men being irate, because God forbid a woman do anything unless it's in response to, or in obstruction of, something a man is doing.

A woman is usually the primary reason for a man's ornery disposition. Specifically, the following are a few things that women are genetically predisposed to doing that make men ill tempered.

NAGGING

Any time a man wants to kick back and start enjoying himself, he can be guaranteed that some cranky hag will come along and stink up the place with her foul bitching. Women love to nag. They never

Figure 1: One of life's simple pleasures: taking a leak off something tall onto something—or someone—below to assert man's dominion over all he sees.

nag quickly; it's always long, dry, time consuming, drawn out, repetitive, boring, and you usually get the point long before it's over—kind of like this sentence.

There are many things women bitch about,[1] and just as many reasons why they bitch. None of these reasons are good of course; since any end to which nagging is the means can't possibly have been a noble enterprise to begin with.

For example, women are all too eager to remind you of minor hygienic oversights that men happen to have from time to time, like

---

1. As a rule of thumb, everything.

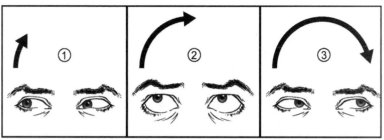

Figure 2: Note the pupils become unfocused as they gaze off to the left corner of the eye (1) just before they start to make the pilgrimage across the optic cavity and toward the ceiling (2), then back down to the opposite side (3) to complete the "rolling" often associated with eyes when women talk for any length of time. Notice the smooth arc, a strong visual indicator that it's time for the woman to cram it.

forgetting to shower. After the second or third week, we get a little tired of hearing about it, so we break down and bathe so she'll finally shut her hole. Brushing our teeth is another big one. Why are women so bent on having us brush our teeth? You think we want to talk to people? Hell no. That's why men don't brush their teeth to begin with, so we can avoid having to talk to people—especially women—any more than is necessary. Men despise talking. In fact, I would be wrtg this entre bk in abrvtins if my edtor wld let me.[2]

Women also love asking us to take out the garbage. Why is this task delegated solely to men? Bitch, how about I take you out? What force is preventing you from getting up off your asses and taking the garbage out yourselves? This same mystical force that drives women's mouths to complain magically disappears when it comes to driving their bodies to do whatever it is they're bitching about in the first place.

Sometimes women nag so much that they don't even realize when they're doing it, in spite of subtle hints. That is to say, men usually give visual cues to a woman to help her realize when she's

2. OPI: Or preferably initials.

doing it. A telltale sign of nagging is when a man's eyes slowly arc across the ceiling (Figure 2), become glazed over, or transfixed on some inanimate point as you talk to us.[3]

RANDOM LOUDNESS

It's hard to say what the most irritable thing a woman could do is, but laughing excessively loud is high up on the list. Here's a rule of thumb: If she has to take in a breath before she laughs, then she's laughing too hard. Everyone has seen this type of woman before; she has a big mouth, lots of teeth, and a fake tan. She laughs so hard that she turns red in the face and gasps for air as if it's the funniest thing she's ever heard, slamming her palm on the table like a primate, sucking in more air with every ear piercing cackle (Figure 3). It's not that funny; nothing is that funny. And while you're at it, you don't need to say "that's hilarious" every time you laugh at something. We know *you* think it's hilarious. Of course, we all know the real reason you're laughing is to gain approval from your friends around you, which is why you turn to look at them to verify that they are laughing along with you.

Sometimes a woman will realize how obnoxious her laughter is by miraculously picking up on the visual cues of glaring bar patrons, but instead of doing something about it, she'll opt instead to excuse it by giving it a name: infectious laughter. This label is fitting, since there's nothing more appropriate to compare this laughter to than a communicable disease.

These spasmodic outbursts of random laughter are cathartic to the groups of women who do it because they desperately seek to grasp this fleeting moment of false happiness to create the illusion of fulfillment

---

3. It's important to note here that women talk *to* us, not *with* us, since those long, rambling monologues women go on hardly constitute a conversation. It's akin to being at church; there's only one person preaching, and we're the ones being preached to. The only major difference is that sermons at church usually don't evoke thoughts of the legal consequences for choking someone to death.

Figure 3: It's called a lounge for a reason, bitch. Calm the fuck down.

in their otherwise vapid lives. These women are starved for attention, and part of the reason they laugh so loud is to get a glance from the men around them. The only problem with their method is that the attention they get from men is like the attention monkeys get at zoos.

CRYING

Men hate it when women cry. It's not that we feel sorry for them, it's that we don't know what to do while they're crying. The amount of comforting a man must feign to make her stop seems completely arbitrary; how much is enough? When women start to cry, men feel trapped. Some men feel like there's something they could be doing to make the woman stop, and they feel obligated to stay until she does. That's why it's important to nip the problem in the bud before it even gets to that point. Here's what you can do to stop a woman from crying before she even starts, or at least minimize the wailing when she does:

- **Have her walk it off.** No feelings can be so wounded that a couple of laps around the block can't fix.
- **Give her ice cream.** All women love comfort foods when they feel down, and those foods are usually fattening. So she'll gain a few more pounds, no big deal. The reason she feels bad in the first place is because you don't want to be seen with her fat ass anyway. Win-win.
- **Tell her to find religion.**
- **Whip out your penis in front of her;** all women are delighted to see a man's genitals. Or at the very least, she'll be concerned that you're thinking of your cock in her time of suffering and she will be too frightened to continue.

One time I dumped a woman, and she didn't take it too well. I told her to stop crying because I only had one roll of toilet paper left. This only made her cry more, so I went downstairs and made myself a sandwich. When she came downstairs to see what I was doing, she had snot running down her nose, so I lost my appetite. Of course, I asked her to reimburse me for the cost of the sandwich that I was no longer going to eat, at which point she exploded even louder. It seemed like no matter what I did, she'd keep crying and begging me to take her back. I finally got tired of it, so I told her that if she took my videos back to the rental store, we could talk. By the time she came back, I had turned off the lights and pretended I wasn't home.

Every time a woman starts to cry, a silent timer starts to tick inside a man's head. As each second passes, the man begins to wonder when it's safe to go back to playing video games. The reason men don't know what to do when women start to cry is because our natural response is to treat the woman like a child; does she want milk? Does she need to be burped? Did she eat something off the floor that upset her stomach? This reaction is natural because adults don't cry. So when an adult does something that a child does, the only suitable response is to treat her like a child.

CHILDREN

If there's one group of people who aren't beat enough these days, it's children. Parents are afraid to beat their kids because of all the social service activists frightening parents shitless with their "psychological scarring" voodoo. The truth is, parents should never beat their children—unless they want their children to behave and grow up well adjusted.

One of the main reasons children make men irate is because they're so arrogant. For example, when children go to fast-food restaurants, they order something made specifically for them called a "kid's meal." There's no such thing as an adult's meal, so children feel important because they get their own exclusive food. This exclusivity makes kids believe that they are significant and that their opinions matter, when in reality this couldn't be further from the truth.

Another reason children are so irritating is because of the double standard with which children are judged. For example, if a three-year-old takes his clothes off at a party and starts running around naked, everyone thinks he's cute. But when I take my clothes off at a party and start running around naked, all I get is complaints such as, "put down the dog" or "I'm calling the police" or "please don't rape us!"

Children have stupid ideas about the world. For example, when the World Trade Center collapsed in 2001, there was an outpouring of support from all around the planet and everyone wanted to share in the redesign process of the new towers, including children. The sheer

Figure 4: What the New York skyline would look like if it were designed by a dipshit.

egotism that a child would need to believe that he or she would be capable of engineering a building is astounding. One candidate, Michael, age five, was even so arrogant as to suggest that the new WTC tower look like his hand with a beak on it (Figure 4).

Rather than reprimanding such brash arrogance, some parents encourage their children by giving them and their foolish ideas undeserved applause. This credence goes straight to a child's head, and the next thing you know, you get kids talking back to parents, exclaiming "no" loudly when they disagree with a rule that the parents have set. They think that they can get away with this because they have their own food, their own television programming, and their own room, so they think that they should have their own opinions as well.

PEOPLE WHO SAY "CIAO" BEFORE THEY HANG UP

Anyone who says "ciao" instead of "bye" or even "later" to end a phone call is an asshole. The only exception is if you're Italian, but even then cool it. Since the subject has been brought up, add "aloha" to that list. I've never met anyone from Hawaii, and I'm not even sure the place exists. Cut the crap, just say "bye" and "hello" like everyone else and save your hep-cat slang for Hollywood.

People who say "ciao" are the same type of people who have those stupid flip phones where the mouth and earpiece pivot on two separate parts. The reason these phones are stupid is because the people who use them go out of their way to make a loud snapping noise as they shut their phone with one hand at the end of every call. It's not the noise that makes men irate so much as the way these people look around the room after the call to see if anyone noticed how cool that one-hand phone snapping bullshit was. Nobody cares, go to hell.

THE ENEMY WITHIN

Sometimes the biggest source of irritation comes from within. Every man must eventually come to terms with his own failure. Every college dropout, fired employee, or middle manager will carry with him the seeds of contempt that will later manifest itself in an angry, vitriolic discharge—sometimes in the form of a book.

is for...
BEEF JERKY

IF SOMEONE INVENTED A WAY TO PACKAGE SEX and put it straight into your mouth, it would taste like beef jerky. When I was six years old, friends and family were shocked when I woke up one day and had a full-grown beard. My voice was deeper, my hands were calloused, and my balls dangled like pendulums. Doctors diagnosed me with precarious puberty—a condition that causes the early onset of puberty. Nobody knew why I was afflicted by this abnormality until they finally traced it to a manliness gene triggered by the manliest food in the universe: beef jerky.

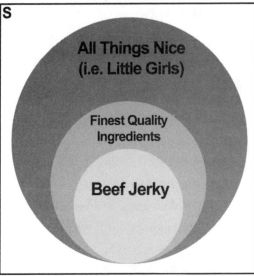

Figure 1: A Venn diagram handing your ass to you.

If there's a food out there that's manlier than strips of flesh ripped from an animal's ribs, cured, smoked, and flavored so it can be slammed down the throats of hungry construction workers, I'd like to know what it is.

Only the highest-quality ingredients go into making beef jerky, but one can't help but wonder: What's the secret ingredient that gives beef jerky its awesome flavor? It's so obvious that it's almost not worth mentioning, but for the benefit of the uninformed: little girls. *Proof:* there's an old nursery rhyme that states, "Little girls are made out of sugar and spice and all things nice." Since only the highest quality ingredients go into making beef jerky, and all things that are of the highest-quality are necessarily a subset of "all things nice," it can be said that beef jerky is made out of little girls (Figure 1). **QED.**

The other major ingredient that goes into making beef jerky is: beef. While some cattle will end up as steaks, and others as uphol-stery in overpriced cars, a cow's greatest aspiration in life is to become jerky, but don't take my word for it.

DIARY OF A COW

What follows is a diary of a cow on a cattle ranch. The diary documents every day the cow lived, but since many of the days contain similar activities, only relevant excerpts are shown here:

JUNE 5, 1989:

I stood around in a field today.

APRIL 12, 1993:

I chewed the grass too deep and accidentally swallowed a rock. I sure am a dumb animal.

APRIL 25, 1998:

It rained this afternoon while we were out in the field. There was a small tin roof covering a portion of the field, but we're too fucking stupid to eat under its cover. Instead, we opted to stand in pouring rain and emit loud moos every time we heard thunder because loud natural sounds that we've heard all our lives still frighten us.

MARCH 16, 2002:

I spelled the word "intangable" wrong in this sentence.

JULY 9, 2003:

It's my birthday today. A couple of guys from the field chipped in and got me dirt.

DECEMBER 22, 2005:

I sure wish I could be eaten.

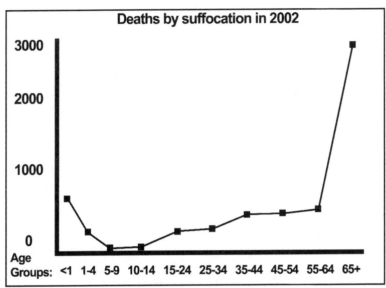

Figure 2

Even in light of authentic testimonials like the one above, some animal rights activists argue that cows are highly intelligent; therefore, we should not eat them. I don't know what the perceived notion of intelligence has to do with whether or not something deserves to be eaten. After all, in 2002 the CDC listed suffocation as one of the ten leading causes of unintentional death in the United States among all age groups. It was the leading cause of death for ages one or below, but to be fair, they're babies and nobody is saying we shouldn't eat them. As you might expect, suffocation as a leading cause of death drops around the age of five to nine, when people normally stop putting plastic bags over their heads (Figure 2).

Notice, however, the sharp increase in fatalities in the age group of sixty-five and older. I should mention that part of the reason this number increases so sharply is because it includes suffocation due to people choking on their own salivary fluid. While it's not as dumb as choking to death on a plastic bag, it's still a pretty stupid way to go. I mean, if something as simple as not swallowing causes your death, you lose your right to live. And yet, animal rights advocates aren't suggesting that it's okay to eat children and old people just because they're stupid.

Still, even moderate activists argue that cows are treated cruelly during their lives. Good point, but there's one small detail they're overlooking: torture makes cows taste bet-

Figure 3: A common wrestling move and an indispensable culinary technique.

ter. I wish someone would make a farm where all the animals were punched, suplexed, and verbally abused as much as possible before consumption (Figure 3). That way, the taste of beef jerky would stay consistently awesome.

 is for...
KNOCKERS

BREASTS ARE WONDERFUL; they can be grabbed, jiggled, sucked on, pressed against windows, pressed against each other, etc. Although knockers are great, one can't help but wonder: Do breasts have any practical use? What would the world be like without them? How have breasts shaped man's evolution?

The role breasts play in man's evolution can perhaps best be explained with the following hypothetical scenarios.

WHAT IF BREASTS RAINED FROM THE SKIES?

Figure 1

The world would be a better place if knockers rained from the sky. After a heavy tit storm, people would run outside and have breast-ball fights, but instead of trying not to be hit, they'd try to catch the tits in their mouths. Children would make breast men instead of snowmen (Figure 1).

Rather than shoveling tits off driveways, people would shovel them into boxes, take them inside, and pour the tits all over themselves.

If it rained breasts, someone would have invented upside-down umbrella pants so none of the breasts would be wasted.

Men would have evolved a mouth on the top of their head to catch the breasts, and an extra mouth on the back of their head just in case they have to tie their shoes during a storm. As wonderful as this utopian world sounds, how dreary would the world be if there were no breasts at all?

WHAT IF THERE WERE NO TITS THROUGHOUT HISTORY?

- Candy wouldn't taste as good.
- Gays wouldn't allow straight marriages.

Figure 2: Without hot Egyptian tits to bang, Alexander the Great doesn't feel like conquering anyone.

- Alexander the Great would have been Alexander the Fuck It (Figure 2).
- The swimming competition in the Olympics would be slightly more tolerable to watch without the breaststroke category.
- We wouldn't need lips.
- Plumbers would wear v-neck pants.
- Women would flash their assholes at rock concerts.
- The G-spot would be in the center of a woman's chest and shaped like a light switch, but men still wouldn't use it.
- Pamela Anderson would still be in Canada.
- Vlad the Impaler would have been Vlad the Masseuse.
- Shakespeare's famous question would have an answer: not to be.

- Martin Luther King would have started and ended his speech with "I have no dream," followed by an awkward silence and uncomfortable small talk as his friends and family tried to avoid bringing up the subject during the drive home.
- Ellen DeGeneres would look exactly the same.

PERSONALITIES

Since the inception of breasts, women have been trying to cast the gloomy shadow of pragmatism on these wonderful organs. These wet blankets downplay their breasts and trivialize them as just being "bags of skin and fat." If you think about it, babies are also just bags of skin and fat, but that doesn't stop women from cradling them.

Thankfully, chest enthusiasts have a more comprehensive classification of breasts that not only takes into consideration the many different styles of boobs but also the personalities of the women who carry them.

TIGHT-ASSED

A telltale sign of a stuck-up bitch is the slightly upturned orientation of her chest (Figure 3). These breasts project themselves outward like daggers, and the angle that the areola subtends can be used as a good indicator of just how much fun you won't be having. The closer the crest comes to forming a right angle with the base, the tighter this woman's ass will become.

Figure 3

For example, if you crack a politically incorrect joke in the workplace, not only will this woman not be laughing, but her colon will clamp shut so tight that you could clip a cigar with it.

COCKY

This woman might as well have a penis, because her rack is almost large enough to compensate for the disadvantage of not having one.

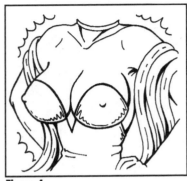

Figure 4

Men who refer to her rack with slang such as "hooters," "milk silos," and "wiener barns" will only do so in jest, as there's only one phrase to accurately describe what her breasts really are: heavenly (Figure 4).

The sheer magnitude of these naturally endowed bosoms will give the woman an especially high sense of self-worth, causing her to become an isolated bitch at parties, talking only to her close group of friends and sexual partners.

SHALLOW

Breasts that appear too perfect to be natural usually are too perfect to be natural. Such is the case with these sculpted hemispheres of synthetic polymers (Figure 5).

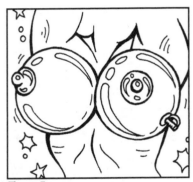

Figure 5

Men have a great deal of respect for physicists like Sir Isaac Newton and his celebrated Newtonian mechanics. We observe the laws of gravity like we observe all laws of nature. The problem with these breasts is that they defy the laws of physics and stand in opposition to man's reverence of these laws. In a sense, they're rebels.

They're "me-too" tits; not quite real, yet real enough to put in your mouth. It's a shame that in their quest to become more sexually desirable, fake-breasted women sacrifice a certain amount of charm and become a muted version of their former selves after the implants.

This dampening of their personalities will result in an overly talkative airheaded version of their former selves, with plenty to talk about, but nothing to say.

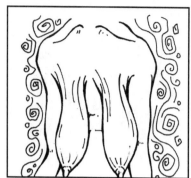

Figure 6

DEPRESSED/CARELESS

The type of personality based on this style of breast isn't as clear-cut as the others. A sagging pair of knockers can mean one of two things: depression or carelessness.

Depression is something that men can deal with because depressed people can be ignored easily. After all, it's not like they'll be getting out of bed to have a debate with you. Carelessness, however, is a symptom of a greater problem: hippies.

Sagging breasts are a sign of caretaker neglect. It's likely that this type of woman holds the point of view that bras are a form of oppression and that wearing one would be a passive acceptance of an oppressive patriarchal regime.

Too bad these hippies will never realize the true purpose of bras: preventing your breasts from becoming long, droopy sacks of veiny skin (Figure 6).

STAGES OF BREAST DEVELOPMENT

Breast selection requires a sharp eye and a good understanding of the different physical features to find those appropriate for your needs. A ripe breast has a sweet fragrance to it, like a hamburger made out of candy.

In selecting a suitable breast, you should look for bruises or scars, color, shape, and texture. Avoid leathery or wrinkly looking skin, as these textures show signs of too much smoking or sun. An ideal breast is medium to large size, as anything too small may have been picked too early, and anything too large will be lumpy and fragile.

KNOCKERS

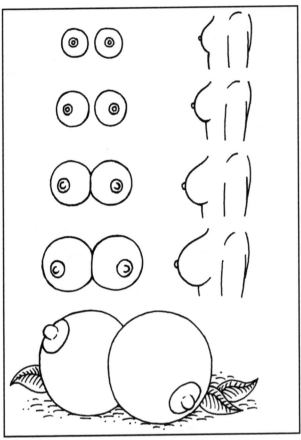

Figure 7

Beware of breasts that are over ripe, as these will be easily bruised and delicate, virtually useless for massaging your penis. It's possible for these breasts to get so large that they will fall off (Figure 7). These breasts will taste terrible and are only suitable for use as pillows.

 is for...

LUMBERJACK

A **LUMBERJACK IS A MAN WHO JACKS LUMBER.** Chopping down trees is all they think about. If there were no trees to chop down, lumberjacks would cease to exist. And yet, lumberjacks have so much contempt for trees that they are willing to sacrifice their very existence to help win the war against nature. Trees are everywhere. It's getting to the point where you can't even go to a park anymore without seeing a tree. If lumberjacks didn't cut down trees, the trees would overwhelm us and take over the world. Then where would we raise our families and park our cars—in the forest? Wishful thinking, and it might even work if it weren't for one small detail: bears.

LUMBERJACK EVOLUTION

Lumberjacks evolved from pirates, and cavemen before that (Figure 1).

Figure 1: The evolution of lumberjacks.

There is no nobler calling than that of a lumberjack. Deep down inside every guy, no matter how much of a pasty-thighed, white-collared desk slave he is, there's a lumberjack waiting to bust out. Not only is being a lumberjack the manliest profession in the world but it's also the only profession to set the definitive style of clothing for men to wear for generations since the first burly lumberjack walked the earth.

LUMBERJACK CLOTHING

PLAID

Lumberjacks wear a distinctive uniform that is both sharp and functional. Unlike the flowery patterns found on wallpaper and women's clothing, lumberjacks have opted for a block-shaped pattern on their clothing called "plaid." The pattern consists of perpendicular bands of color (usually alternating strips of red and black) and clashes with every other style of clothing and color known to man. Though plaid has its critics, even the most ardent opponents are hard pressed to deny that a plaid shirt has an underspoken classiness to it.

Plaid is unapologetically manly because it stands diametrically opposed to all shapes and patterns found in nature. Things in nature tend to be organic and unorganized. Plaid stands in sharp contrast, being rigid and calculated. It's a subtle nod toward man's ability to rationalize and think.

YOU DON'T KNOW JACK

While there's a fair amount that we know about lumberjacks, there are almost as many things that we don't know about them. For example, why are lumberjacks so hairy? Is there anything a lumberjack won't eat? How many ice skaters would a lumberjack have to karate chop before he got bored? Many of these questions will perhaps always remain unanswered, but there are a few things we do know.

TRANSPORTATION

The primary mode of transportation for a lumberjack is by bull. While ordinary bulls eat grass and antibiotics, a lumberjack's bull feeds on endangered species (see Figure 2, opposite).

The reason their bulls are fed endangered species is because lumberjacks are proponents of ecological diversity. There are only two major groups in the animal kingdom: endangered species and nonendangered species. If endangered species were allowed to procreate and reestablish their populations as they please, then they would no longer be endangered, and the only kind of animal we'd have left is the plain old nonendangered kind. So we would lose an entire category of animals, leaving us only one, and having only one category isn't diverse by any measure of the imagination.

Figure 2

WHERE DO LUMBERJACKS COME FROM?

Even though lumberjacks evolved from pirates, the ruggedness they exhibit isn't so much inherited as it is imbued. Lumberjacks are raised by Cyclopses and learn all they need to know by the age of two (Figure 3).

I'm not really going anywhere with this. I just think Cyclopses are cool, and there's really nowhere else in the book I could mention them.

Figure 3

CONVERSATIONS WITH MY SISTER

My sister thinks I'm an idiot for caring so much about lumberjacks, so she interviewed me for a report she was doing.

HER: Who cares about lumberjacks?

ME: Me.

HER: Why do you care about lumberjacks?

ME: Because they're manly.

HER: But it's just a profession. What's so special about someone who cuts down trees every day?

ME: No, being a lumberjack isn't a profession, it's who they are. People are born lumberjacks, like you're born a moron.

HER: Why do you think they're manly?

ME: Because they chop down trees and they're hairy. They wear plaid.

HER: I don't think they're manly. I think they're stupid. They cut down trees by using their muscle instead of their brains. That's why they're stupid.

ME: You can't cut down trees with brains. You need an axe.

After I learned how she felt about lumberjacks, I called her nazi bitch.

 is for...
METAL

IF MANLINESS HAD A SOUNDTRACK, the score would be metal. No other genre of music is in jeopardy of dying out because its fans keep getting killed at concerts. Decades ago, angry menstruating moms and fanatical Christian conservatives tried to get metal banned for being a bad influence on our youth. They claimed that metal caused harm to children and caused violent behavior in adolescents. Today we know for a fact that they were right.

Metal causes pain, suffering, hatred, and is probably the cause of more than one miscarriage. Everything about metal falls in two categories: dangerous or vulgar. If it doesn't threaten your well-being, it's sure to offend someone. Take for example the horn hand sign at the top of this section. It's a vul-

Figure 1: Do not stick your thumb out. This is the symbol for "love," which has nothing to do with getting rocked.

gar gesture made by first creating a fist, then extending your index and little fingers out while holding the middle two fingers with your thumb. Not to be confused with the symbol for "love" (Figure 1).

I remember the first time I came home from a heavy metal concert when I was nine. I couldn't sleep for two months. It ruined my life. The music was so loud that it gave my friend back problems. I couldn't believe how much it ruled. It was then that I knew that metal was the only music I'd ever listen to again.

Rock historians often try to connect classical influences with metal in a strained attempt to make heavy metal seem more complex and sophisticated. They talk about the sociopolitical statements the lyrics make, using fancy words like "dichotomy" to describe the impact metal has on our culture. I don't even want to know what "dichotomy" means. I've never used that word in my life, except in the last two sentences. These forced references and $6 words are made in an attempt to legitimize metal as an art form.

I don't want metal to become more legitimate; I want it to become less legitimate. Metal isn't made by a bunch of guys discussing the subtleties of fifteenth-century melodic form; it's made by a bunch of dudes with heroine addictions and bad haircuts. Part of what makes metal rule so hard is the aggressive mannerisms associated with it.

HEADBANGERS

Headbanging is the act of banging your head in synch with a particularly heavy riff. Headbangers who practice this act too violently have been known to suffer from whiplash, brain damage, and fatalities. No other genre of music requires you to die in order to enjoy it fully.

HOW TO HEADBANG

Though it might seem pretty straightforward, there are several headbanging schools of thought out there. The first method is the most common, sometimes called the "jackhammer" method. This requires long hair to do effectively, so if you don't have shoulder-length Thor-like hair, grow some. If you happen to be bald, you may still partake in this ritual so long as you also have a bitchin' tattoo on a noticeable part of your body—something like a shark, or a skull, or a skull shark, preferably on your face. Here are the steps for the jackhammer technique:

STEP 1: Whip your head back as far as it can go, like you're about to sneeze or cough in someone's face. Make sure you have a mean expression as you do this so that everyone will know that you're in the business of kicking ass, and business is good (Figure 2).

Figure 2

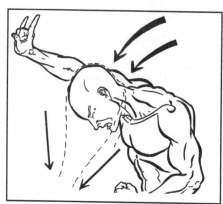

Figure 3

STEP 2: When you reach the height of your charge, whip your head down in the opposite direction. Make sure to go straight down so that your hair is thrust into a perfect cone below you (Figure 3). You're also encouraged to make the horn gesture with your hand for full effect.

Another way to headbang is to swirl your head around in circles, also known as the "windmill" method. While it's not as potentially debilitating as the jackhammer, nor as readily recognized, it's still an acceptable form of headbanging (Figure 4)

Figure 4: The circular motion makes you look like you're possessed, which is highly desirable, and may make up for this style's intrinsic hokeyness.

The problem with the windmill method is that it's corny. It's what hippy women did in the '60s during transitions on the dreadful variety shows that our parents reminisce so fondly about. This was back when the world was more innocent and books like this didn't exist to give our lives meaning.

Finally, there's one other headbanging style worth mentioning that involves banging your head from side to side horizontally. This is called the "poser" method, also sometimes referred to as the "hey, look at that jackass" style. The reason the "hey, look at that jackass" style is looked down upon is because if you have long hair—and you should—waving it from side to side will inevitably get you tangled with someone else, and trying to untangle your hair with another man is probably one of the unmanliest things you can do. Just say no.

MOSHING

So you're at a metal concert, the band is thrashing your ass off, the ringing in your ears is so loud that people around you can hear it, but what can you be doing other than headbanging while you stand around? Simple: you pick a fight, or "mosh" as it's sometimes called.

Moshing is typically done in an area of the concert floor called the "mosh pit." There are two types. The first, and most common, is the circular pit (see Figure 5, top of next page). A group of guys go nuts and start pushing each other around, clearing a circle where they can punch each other to their hearts' content. The second type is the box pit, an area near the front of the stage that spans from one wall to the other and is separated by a wall of onlookers (Figure 6).

Once you've either created a mosh pit, or a mosh pit has been created around you, there are a few techniques you can learn to help you become a more effective mosher.

METAL

Figure 5: The circle pit.

Figure 6: The box configuration, sometimes called the "blood box." Fights here typically last longer and are more violent than in the circle pit.

THE HUMAN JAVELIN: First spot a short, skinny- looking guy (the bonier he is, the better). Then pick him up and toss that fucker toward a group of people like a javelin (Figures 7–8). Props if you're able to toss him through someone. It's best to have the cooperation of a buddy, so he can clap his hands together like a spear for more effective penetration.

Figure 7: Pick him up.

Figure 8: Toss that fucker!

LIKELIHOOD YOU'LL GET YOUR ASS KICKED: 10 percent if you're the one doing the tossing since people usually don't see it coming and don't know the source, and 90 percent if you're the one being tossed since you'll probably break your neck, but don't be a wuss, take one for the team.

POSER BOWLING: Every once in a while there will be a group of kids at a metal concert who will forget where they are and show up wearing emo rags. Though they might be metal fans as well, the emo attire is inappropriate and should set off your poser detector. The best way to break the group up is to pack yourself in a ball shape and have a strong buddy of yours roll you into the group, knocking the posers over like skinny angst-filled bowling pins. An alternative method would be to have a buddy stuff you into a garbage can, then roll the can into them.

LIKELIHOOD YOU'LL GET YOUR ASS KICKED: 0 percent, posers won't fight back. Instead, they'll drift to the back of the room so they can sulk while they drink warm beer.

NO JOKE BACKHAND: Metal rocks, but occasionally someone will enjoy it too much. He'll be way too enthusiastic, jumping up and down like a jackass in between songs. It's best to dispatch him with a swift backhand. Just get up close to him, stand about a foot behind so you'll have room to carry through with your swing, then crack that son of a bitch right in the mouth with the backside of your hand. The impact should be strong enough to knock him on his ass, and then he will know you're not joking around.

METAL

METAL

Figure 9: You won't find Israelites following this fatass across Egypt.

LIKELIHOOD YOU'LL GET YOUR ASS KICKED: 50 percent, it's a coin toss since the cause of his enthusiasm might be too much alcohol, or he could just be plain old vanilla crazy, in which case he might try to cut you.

THE FLYING MOSES: This is what you call a fat person who tries to crowd surf. Even before he jumps, people take note of him and keep him in mind so that when his turn comes up, they can get the hell out of the way. When he finally goes airborne, the crowd will part like the Red Sea (Figure 9). The result will be one fat bastard getting well acquainted with the cold, hard floor.

LIKELIHOOD YOU'LL GET YOUR ASS KICKED: 100 percent, gravity wins this one.

THE BATTERING RAM: Get a couple of strong buddies together and decide who will be the battering ram. If you can't decide, go with the person who objects the most. Next, you and your buddy each grab an arm and a leg and charge into the crowd. Try to knock as many people over as possible.

LIKELIHOOD YOU'LL GET YOUR ASS KICKED: 80 percent, you're guaranteed to piss off a lot of people, and you will break a few limbs (probably your own). Awesome.

Though moshing has its roots at metal concerts, it doesn't have to be limited to this venue. Here are some other occasions you can mosh:

- **WEDDINGS**
- **BABY SHOWERS**
- **BARMITZVAHS**
- **PLAYGROUNDS (FIGURE 10)**

- **FUNERALS**
- **GRADUATIONS**
- **PEACE VIGILS**

METAL

Figure 10

Be creative, don't let convention stop you from ruining someone's celebration.

ETIQUETTE—
THE DO'S AND DON'TS OF METAL

DO NOT STRUT LIKE A CHICKEN: It makes you look like an idiot. There's always at least one guy doing this, maybe two, but no more (I think it's a territorial thing). Everyone has seen this guy before; he's the skinhead who takes his shirt off and walks around in a circle, puffing his chest out and cocking his head back and forth like a chicken, staring people down like his ass is bullet proof (Figure 11). I don't know where this started or why it has caught on, but it has to stop.

DO NOT TAKE OFF YOUR SHIRT: Let's get one thing straight: you have a day job, you drive a compact sedan, and you eat cereal high in fiber because you're concerned about your cholesterol. There are only two reasons for you to take off your shirt during any other day of the week, and neither of them involves sex. Nobody is impressed, just put the shirt back on and hope that nobody noticed.

HARDCORE DANCING IS STUPID: If you're not familiar with the phenomenon, good. Hardcore dancing is the act of punching and kicking the air or the ground as hard as you can. Yes, seriously. Imagine what it would look like if a kung-fu master danced at a metal concert. Now imagine that same kung-fu master without any skill, discipline, or basic hand-eye coordination, and you have hardcore dancing.

Thankfully, hardcore dancing bouts usually don't last very long

Figure 11: Skinheads—not celebrated for their innovative dance technique.

because the participants tire themselves out after a few minutes like four-year-olds on a candy rush.

DO NOT SPIT UNLESS YOU'RE ON STAGE: This one should be self-explanatory, but just in case you're not familiar with a metal crowd, everyone is to assume that everyone else around them has herpes.

TAKE A SHOWER: I don't think there ever has been, or ever will be, a person interested in finding out what you smell like after a twelve-hour shift at Home Depot. If you don't have time to shower before the show, try to shower at least the week of the concert. If you smell like cheese before you go, you're going to smell even worse once you're at the concert getting beer spilled on you. Taking your shirt off will amplify the smell, making it unbearable for those around you, causing two things: (1) their eyes to water and (2) your ass to get kicked.

DON'T SHOUT SONGS AT THE BAND: They know what they're going to play next, and they don't need a vocal cue from Joe Nobody to remind them of the songs at their disposal. Also, if you happen to guess correctly which song they play next, shut the fuck up about it. You're not on some higher level of consciousness than everybody else;

you don't have a "connection" with the band. Nobody cares if you got the song right. Hey, you know what's even better than hearing you talk about how you "knew" which song they were going to play? Hearing the song.

If your friend passes out, call for help immediately: not because you care, but because you don't want to be associated with such a pussy, and people might remember that the two of you came in together.

GUITAR PICKS ARE THE MOST VALUABLE THINGS IN THE UNIVERSE: At any other time or place, a guitar pick is absolutely worthless, but thrown from the hand of a guitarist, those picks become the most valuable objects in the universe. Fighting for guitar picks is expected and encouraged; you may draw blood if necessary, so long as you have a worthless souvenir to show for it. Getting kicked out of the concert and possibly arrested for assault is a small price to pay for a thin piece of plastic. Besides, when you're sitting in jail later that night, you'll have something to play with as you contemplate which inmate is going to rape you.

WHAT TO WEAR

PLAIN BLACK OR PLAIN WHITE T-SHIRT: Don't try to stand out. Any other colors—including gray—are too cheerful. Red is sometimes acceptable, but only if it's someone else's blood on your shirt.

T-SHIRTS WITH OFFENSIVE SLOGANS: A rule of thumb is that if you've worn it around your family and you haven't been excommunicated yet, it's probably not offensive enough.

WIFE BEATERS: A wife beater is sometimes okay to wear, but it depends on what you wear with it. For example, if you wear a cowboy hat, it's too white trash. It's not that the shirt doesn't fit in at a metal concert; it's just that it fits in so much better with country music, where there's no such thing as *too white trash*.

NO TRENCH COATS: Trench coats are creepy, but not in a good way. Guys who wear trench coats to concerts are naked underneath nine times out of ten.

THE METAL EFFECT

Sadly, the popularity of the metal genre has waned over the years, partly due to the high mortality rate of its fan base, and partly due to the rise in popularity of butt-rock. Fortunately it's not too late to reverse the course of this decline; here's what you can do to make your children take interest in metal at an early age.

Many people are becoming familiar with the "Mozart Effect," a theory that suggests that playing classical music for your baby while still in the womb may help build neural connections and increase the baby's IQ, as well as having other positive effects such as strengthening relationships with the family. While it sounds like horseshit, there are some studies that suggest that there might be some truth to this theory.

If there's credence to this theory, then it's also possible to have a "Metal Effect": the theory that playing metal for your baby while still in the womb may decrease the baby's IQ, as well as having other positive effects such as causing your child to stomp more ass.

The only problem with this theory is that it might be hard to get your woman to cooperate by playing metal for the baby in utero. But

METAL

there is something you can do to preempt your bitch wife from ruining your kids: blast your balls with metal (Figure 12)! She can't get knocked up without your sperm, so you can rock your balls off to your heart's content before she has a chance to turn your kids into pussies—and there's nothing she can do about it. The beauty of it is that she won't even know until it's too late. Just hold the speakers up to your nuts and blast that metal as loud as you can, several times per day. The Metal Effect should cause lasting damage and ensure that your kids will be the meanest sons o' bitches on the block.

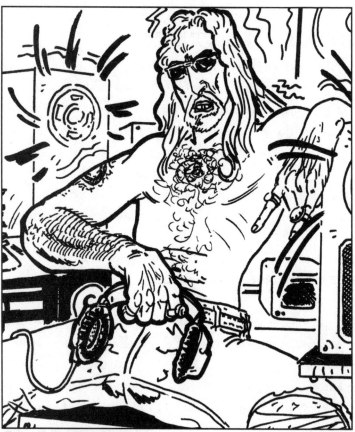

Figure 12: The Metal Effect.

is for...
CHUCK NORRIS

CHUCK NORRIS EATS ROCKS and shits lightning bolts. One time Chuck Norris was walking around in the forest, looking for hippies to use as firewood, when a wild boar suddenly crossed his path. Big mistake. Chuck lifted the boar into the air with his mind, spun him around, and digested him telekinetically. And Chuck wasn't even hungry.

If you don't know who Chuck Norris is, he's the world champion in tae kwon do, jujutsu, kickboxing, karate, sumo wrestling, tae bo, pad thai, *Street Fighter II*, and he holds a certificate of participation in the national spelling bee. Chuck Norris has no weakness; he is the ultimate fighting machine. One time, a big shot movie producer approached Chuck Norris with a screenplay starring him versus King Kong, Gidorah, Dracula, Satan, Charles Bronson, and that Russian boxer from *Rocky IV*. The movie was never made though because studios felt that it was too far fetched, since nobody but nobody stands a chance against Chuck Norris. When Chuck found out, he was so furious that the producer had to offer his daughter's virginity to appease him. Chuck accepted the offer and then torched the producer's family in their sleep. The producer wrote Chuck a "thank you" letter for sparing his life, which Chuck promptly crumpled up and urinated on.

Speaking of film, here is a transcript of a conversation a producer had with Chuck regarding his asking cost for a film:

> **CHUCK NORRIS:** $100 billion dollars.
> **PRODUCER:** How about $20 million?
> **CHUCK NORRIS:** . . . (see Figure 1)

THE HISTORY OF CHUCK

Not much is known about Chuck Norris's childhood. Chuck Norris has no mother, as crawling out of a vagina is unbecoming of a man of his stature. Chuck spontaneously came into existence on Karl Marx's birthday. This was no coincidence since Chuck Norris is the polar opposite of communism; he is the yang to communism's yin, and the very thought of a political theory that suggests that people should have their own means of production in a classless society makes Chuck Norris want to puke.

Chuck Norris has fought in almost every major war, including the Korean War, World War I, the American Civil War, the Peloponnesian

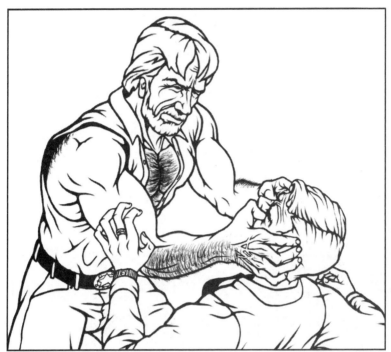

Figure 1: Chuck Norris displacing a producer's eyes with his thumbs.

War, the Iran-Iraq War (on both sides simultaneously), the War of the Worlds, and the War on Drugs. The only war Chuck hasn't fought in is the Macedonian war because Chuck Norris doesn't give a shit about Macedonia. Chuck Norris wins wars by attrition.

Here is a list of Chuck's favorite foods:

- **WHISKEY**

Sometimes when Chuck gets tired of whiskey, he'll eat bread, cheese, some tomato paste and a handful of basil, which sounds like pizza, but it's not because Chuck Norris doesn't want to give the Italians the credit. Every now and then, Chuck Norris will sit down and eat an entire plate of sausage and onions for no reason.

ENCOUNTERS WITH CHUCK

One time I went to Chuck Norris's house on Halloween, and I dressed up like a pussy because you're supposed to dress like something you're not, and I figured that Chuck Norris would appreciate ironic humor. I walked up a winding pathway to his house, which was a giant floating volcano with American bald eagles flying around it, and with a long staircase leading to the top (Figure 2).

I walked up the staircase for what seemed like days, and when I finally reached the top, I saw Chuck Norris sitting on his throne. I dared not look him in his eyes because one time this guy looked him

Figure 2: Chuck's revered abode.

in his eyes and Chuck Norris spontaneously combusted him. No one is allowed to speak with Chuck; the only thing you are allowed to do in his presence is bow, kiss his ring, bow again, and leave. So I walked up to his throne and saw that he was wearing a ring made out of solid diamonds with a uni- corn on it that had an erec- tion (Figure 3).

Figure 3: I'd have a boner too if I were on Chuck Norris's ring.

NORRIS, CHUCK

I kissed his ring, and then I wanted to thank him, so I said, "Sir, permission to thank you for the privilege of allowing me to kiss your ring." If Chuck Norris doesn't immediately kill you, that means he has granted you permission. I thanked him, bowed, and left. It was the happiest day of my life.

I once had a friend who claimed that he went over to Chuck Norris's house and hung out with him. I didn't believe him, so I asked him for proof and he told me that Chuck Norris owns the complete *Back to the Future* trilogy on laser disc. I was so jealous that I called him a liar, but deep inside I knew he was telling the truth.

A DAY IN THE LIFE OF CHUCK NORRIS

The word "day" is a bit misleading when talking about Chuck Norris because a day in his life is less like the twenty-four-hour day most peo- ple associate with the word, and more like an eon God describes as a day during creation of the universe:

Chuck Norris starts his day like every red-blooded man: with a giant boner. After rubbing one off, Chuck flosses his teeth with steel wool. Then he eats a bowl of dynamite, takes a massive two-flush megashit, and wipes his ass with intercepted letters to Santa Claus.

After breakfast, Chuck brings in his mail and uses the Spear of Destiny as an envelope opener. Chuck Norris not only stays up to date on current events but future ones as well so that he can ruin the ending to new *Harry Potter* books before they're even written.

One time, Chuck Norris read a news piece about some guy who was given a death penalty for treason. Treason is especially offensive to Chuck because he embodies everything that is, was, or ever will be American. Chuck Norris loves America so much that when he gets interrupted during sex, he gets red, white, and blue balls. So when Chuck read about this traitor, he killed himself, went to hell and ripped the guy's face off and uses it as a loincloth to this day. Chuck then resurrected himself, went to lunch, and paid for his food using exact change.

In the evening, Chuck Norris likes to sit in the dark and silently pray that his enemies get cancer.

Thus concludes a day in the life of the greatest American ever to live.

is for...
OBEDIENCE

HAVING AN OBEDIENT WIFE, and kids who flinch and hide in the corner of the room when you come home is the hallmark of a successful family. Since having a well-tempered wife is essential to asserting one's manliness, here is a quick guide to finding and training your new wife.

WHERE TO FIND A WOMAN

Bringing a woman into your home is a life-altering decision that requires careful consideration. Before you make the financial, social, and time commitment to adopt a woman, ask yourself if you're ready for the ongoing responsibility. Once you've decided that a woman is right for you, the first step is to find one. Here are a few places to start your search:

MALLS

Most women can be found in malls—large shopping establishments that can be found in most major cities. Malls are rife with idle women ready for the picking. You can find women of different builds depending on which area of the mall you look in. For example, looking in trendy or novelty clothing stores will yield a younger, valley-girl type of woman, whereas if you look in the food court, you will usually find a larger breed of woman with thicker thighs that are more suitable for birthing.

SCHOOLS

College campuses are a great resource for men in the market for women who come fixed. Females on university campuses are likely to be in heat, in good health, and anxious to leave the confinement of their self-imposed academic prisons. Since stock models of these women come sterile, they're ideal for men who are looking to avoid undesirable sexually transmitted diseases.[1]

BARS/CLUBS

If women are like steaks, then the big greasy chunks of gristle that are left over after you finish the meal are what you'll find in bars. Fortunately, there is a way to separate out the high-quality women

1. Namely, children

from the low in bars and clubs. When you stand near a woman, listen for a faint whistling noise coming from between her legs, as if wind were passing through a large, hollow cavern. If you hear this sound, your prospective woman may have a condition commonly referred to as "whore." Be wary of these women, as clubs tend to harbor many of them.

TYPES OF WOMEN

Once you find an establishment with women, the next step is to choose a woman that's right for you based on your level of commitment. Surprisingly, not all women are the same; that is, women can vary greatly in intelligence, body type, and personality. The following is a list of the most common classifications of women.

BLONDES: This type of woman is energetic and enthusiastic. These personality traits will wear thin after a couple of minutes and will transform into another personality trait known as "annoying." Blondes love to laugh, drink, and hang out in bars, and as such have a propensity to be loose. Women with blond hair tend to have overtanned skin and blue eyes, which are seen as desirable physical traits by some men. This desirability is fueled by the music and television industries; so this type of woman is greatly sought after. Some analysts believe that, due to overvaluation, the market for blondes is about to burst.

BRUNETTES: As a rule of thumb, brunettes are more meek than their blonde counterparts, due to the higher perceived value of blondes. This underlying devaluation will occasionally manifest itself as "low self-esteem," making brunettes more easily attainable. Unfortunately, not all brunettes are desirable, and the exceptions can be tragic. For example, the brunettes with lighter skin tend to sport especially noticeable moustaches, due to the dark color of their hair follicles. This type of woman may require a high level of maintenance to keep presentable.

REDHEADS: Redheads require a very assertive owner due to the trying natures of these women. For instance, most redheads are very combative with other women and even some men if you allow it to happen. The dominant nature of this breed may be undesirable to men with flimsy backbones.

NEW OWNER CHECKLIST

After you select a woman, it's important to go through the following checklist to make sure she is right for you:

- Is the woman's body clean and well trimmed? Are her upper-lip, shoulders, and lower back clear of hair?
- Any unusual smells? For that matter, any "usual" smells?
- Any excess baggage? This could be fat, kids, or psychological issues.
- Does she have black fingernails, nappy looking hair, scar tissue around her wrists, bags under her eyes, or creepy pink thigh-high stockings? (All these say "head case." Be wary, these women can be exhilarating at times, but you're just as likely to have your penis cut off in your sleep.)
- Are her shots and vaccinations current?
- Does she walk with a limp?
- Does she look like she's been bred more than twice?
- Did you check to make sure she's not wearing flip-flops?

BRINGING YOUR WOMAN HOME

There are several preparations you need to make before bringing your woman home. This is done for the safety of your property and belongings, as well as to prevent any unexpected medical bills due to accidental ingestion of drugs or toxic substances that may be in your home.

THE KITCHEN

If left unsupervised, you will find that most women will naturally find their way to the kitchen. Although your kitchen may appear to be safe at first, there are several potential risks that you need to be aware of. The most common accidents occur when pot handles are left hanging over the edge of the stove. Make sure to turn the handles toward the back of the stove, where she will be less likely to knock them over while she's mopping the floors.

THE BATHROOM

Make sure to keep medicine and supplements locked in cabinets. Some women have occasional fits of depression and may attempt to get attention by swallowing half a bottle of Tylenol. While this rarely poses a threat to the woman's safety, Tylenol is expensive.

One exception to this rule can be made with Midol, which you should leave in a candy dish in plain sight at least once per month. This will help keep your woman's irritability in check. If you find that your woman is not consuming the Midol, you may consider mixing crushed tablets into her food.

BATHING TIPS: It's important never to leave your woman alone in the tub, lest she slip and drown. Always stay with your woman while she's in the tub; you may even consider joining her. A long day of cooking and cleaning will make a woman filthy, so make sure to run an extra hot bath or shower, and scrub behind

OBEDIENCE

her ears and between her breasts—especially between her breasts. A woman's chest is the filthiest part on her body and needs extra scrubbing to clean. Sometimes scrubbing isn't enough, so you must use your mouth on her nipple pores to thoroughly clean your woman.

EXERCISE AND DIET

All women require some level of exercise and diet to keep fit and presentable. How much exercise a woman requires depends on several factors, including her body weight, frame, chest size, and self-esteem. For example, a woman with a low self-esteem will tend to overeat, causing her more weight gain than a woman with higher self-esteem.

Women with large busts require a type of exercise that consists of jogging, skipping, or jumping up and down on a trampoline. These types of exercise will help you determine your woman's chest pliability. Some women with breast augmentations may show signs of discomfort while doing these exercises, in which case you should promptly exchange her for a natural model that won't suffer from boulder tit syndrome.

Managing your woman's diet won't be simple, but can be accomplished by giving her less food. If your woman seems irritable with less food, try supplementing her meals with unflattering comments about her hips and thighs. Failing that, you may need to bring another woman into the picture; nothing makes a woman shape up like the threat of another woman vying for your attention. With practice, you'll find that a woman's jealousy can be used like a tool to manipulate her into doing all sorts of things to gain your praise.

It's also important to feed your woman high-quality food to prevent infections and other undesirable effects such as upset stomach, diarrhea, and bitching. Feeding her filler foods (i.e., Taco Bell) may cause parasites to invade her body. If you suspect that this is the case, have a stool sample checked for worms by a qualified physician.

HOUSE TRAINING YOUR WOMAN

Upon bringing your woman home, house training should be one of your top priorities. The key to effective house training is implementing a reward-counterreward system to encourage good behavior and discourage bad behavior.

A great deal of supervision and patience is required while training your woman to relieve herself properly. She may complain about finding the toilet seat up, but she will eventually learn that she can put the toilet seat down with a fraction of the energy she'd expend complaining about it.

You should reward her good behavior by giving her treats such as flowers (keep your eye out for half-off sales, or if you don't mind carnations, stop by a cemetery), TV allowances that she can use to watch her favorite shows when you're not home, and if you're feeling particularly generous, you could let her take you out to dinner instead of cooking for you.

If an accident should occur, you must exercise care not to overdo your punishment while still sending her a message that this is unacceptable behavior. Make sure that whatever command you say will be simple enough for her to remember easily.

These tips taken together will help make your ownership experience a good one.

 **is for...**
PIRATES

A **LONG TIME AGO,** back when men were men and having a hairy back was a sign of virility, there was a breed of man that was saltier, meaner, and more spiteful than all the rest. This specimen of masculinity stood apart from the peasants and pansies of the day who saturated every unexploited seaport. Today, pirates stand as a monument of anger and ill temperament triumphing over cool-headedness and positive emotions.

For those deficient in piratical knowledge, that is, you, here are some facts about pirates:

- The only thing that can kill a pirate is another pirate.
- Pirates drink rum almost exclusively. The only exception is for an occasional iced mocha or chai tea with 2 percent milk.
- Pirates prefer BBQ- or Cajun-flavored potato chips.
- A pirate's sweat tastes like whiskey.
- Sometimes pirates kick cats just because.
- Pirates think college is a waste of time.
- Eye patches make chicks horny.
- Pirates possess parrots with eye patches and pirated prosthetic peg legs.
- A pirate's semen is indestructible.
- Pirates hate all forms of dancing, except for break dancing, which lumberjacks would agree is awesome.
- All pirates have hair on their backs and knuckles. Women find this intriguing.
- A pirate ejaculates fully-grown leprechauns (Figure 1).

You might have a few questions on your mind about this list, like "if the only thing that can kill a pirate is another pirate, then where are all the pirates today?" Simple: People stopped believing in them.

It's easy to stop believing in pirates in

Figure 1

this world of micro-processors and MP3 ring tones, but if you believe hard enough, you'll see that pirates haven't really disappeared at all. They're all around us; doing your taxes, writing your legacy file migration software, and answering your customer service calls.

Figure 2

Though pirates may permeate every facet of society, a pirate's cultural assimilation doesn't come easily, and pirates often find themselves frustrated when adapting to modern inconveniences and social norms. Thankfully, pirates can rely on other pirates to help make this transition a smooth one.

Figure 3

HOW TO SURVIVE AS A PIRATE IN THE MODERN WORLD

• DO NOT THROW FAX MACHINES

Fax machines are relics of the '70s when the thought of sharing documents with colleagues miles away seemed novel. Unfortunately, this archaic contrivance persists in light of newer technology that has emerged over the years, namely e-mail.

The sound of a fax machine startles and annoys pirates, and a pirate's first impulse may be to take the source of his frustration and throw it out the window (see Figure 2, opposite). This is not proper office etiquette, and may result in peer review. Likewise, the dispatching of other annoyances such as gabby co-workers in a similar fashion is also perceived negatively in the work place (Figure 3).

• STABBING THE WAIT STAFF IS LOOKED DOWN UPON

While at work, a pirate may occasionally find himself invited to informal get-togethers, where he and his co-workers will eat food

Figure 4: Cutting the wait staff is discourteous.

and partake in trivial conversations about politics and other such topics they know little about.

During this gathering, or "lunch," one might experience dissatisfaction with the quality of the meal or the diligence of the wait staff, and may wish to take issue with him or her. Though it may be consistent with a pirate's nature to stab or assault the server (see Figure 4, previous page), it is considered ill mannered. A more appropriate way of handling the situation would be to inform the waiter or waitress of the problem and try to resolve the matter without the aid of a cutlass.

•IT IS NOT POLITE TO RAPE

This is a big one. One of the more difficult adjustments for a pirate to make while transitioning into society is that rape is not "okay." In fact, rape is considered rude and is sharply frowned upon (Figure 5).

The proper way to consummate a relationship with a woman is to ask her out, spend $50 on the first date, go home with blue balls, call

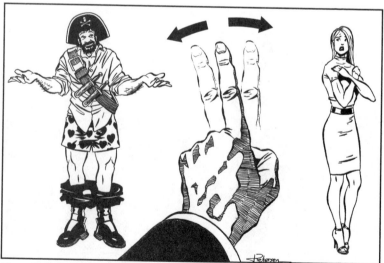

Figure 5: Rape is a social gaffe.

her the next day and pretend that you had a good time, schedule a follow-up date, go over to her house to pick her up only to realize that she invited her ugly friend to tag along, take her friend home early because she got drunk and passed out, then drop your woman off because she has to "go to work early" the next morning, awkwardly shuffle your feet on her front step as you wait for her to pull her head out of her ass and give you some lip action, call her again the next day and invite her over for pizza and a movie—which really means sex—and seal the deal when she dashes for your crotch.

• PILLAGING AND PLUNDERING ARE NOT OKAY UNLESS DONE UNDER A CORPORATE FACADE

Gone are the days when pirates would walk into people's homes, eat all their food, try on some clothes, and take a handful of silverware or panties and leave. Sadly, the only form of theft that's tolerated in society is white-collar theft that executives commit every day by robbing shareholders blind of their fortunes. But don't worry, even though the stakes are high, you don't have to worry about serving any time if you get caught because tossing a few bills toward a powerful politician's election fund goes a long way toward getting you out of the slammer.

• PUTTING YOUR MONEY IN A BANK WILL USUALLY YIELD HIGHER INTEREST RATES THAN BURYING IT

The key word in this rule is "usually," since it's possible that you'll find greater returns on your investment after you dig it up. After all, earthworms can be used for fishing, and fish are delicious.

That about covers the basics. There are other rules that pirates should abide by when trying to become naturalized into society, but unfortunately they lie outside the scope of this book.

PIRATES

is for...
QUICKIE

THE ONLY THING WORSE THAN FOREPLAY is after-play. For the uninitiated, afterplay is defined as anything that comes after sex that doesn't involve her leaving. More specifically: cuddlng, talking, kissing, necking, spooning, holding hands, eating (food), showering, and possibly the worst of all—looking into each other's eyes.

Women love the "quickie" because it makes them feel useful. The thing to keep in mind is that a quickie is all about you, and most women are content with being a perfunctory part of your experience. Some women complain about the quickie because they can't climax in only a few minutes. While this may be true, quickies can be just as rewarding for the women involved if you're a classy enough guy to follow through. For example, if you want to show a woman how much you appreciate her, try writing her a check. When she wakes up alone, she'll see that you value her.

Another way to help a reluctant woman appreciate the quickie is to use your voice to lull her into a sopping wet sexual frenzy.

The problem with talking to a woman to get her "in the mood" is that it's dangerously close to foreplay, and it might give her the impression that you appreciate her idle conversation. What's worse is that you might have to say the same things over and over to different women all throughout your life. Thankfully, there is a solution: the tape recorder. You can give a tape to as many women as you want, but you only have to make one recording. Just make sure the recording is general enough so that it applies to all the women you could possibly bang.

SAMPLE SCRIPT:

Hey baby, did I ever tell you how sexy your brown or blue eyes look? The other day when I saw you at school or the grocery store or whatever, you looked horny. I know how bad you want me. You want me to take you home and sit on your face. Yeah. You like that baby? Guess what I'm touching right now? Three inches of solid dynamite.

[*Pause for music: it should be something that will get her in the mood to procreate, like flamenco.*]

If you like what you're hearing, why don't you give me a call and leave me a message with your name, phone number, and what time would be good for you to *come*[1] over for a quickie.

This tape gets them every time. In fact, here's a transcript of the response my girlfriend left on my voicemail:

1. Make sure to emphasize the word "come" so she knows that you're clever enough to point out your puns.

START MESSAGE

> I found another one of your tapes on my dresser this morning. This is really starting to creep me out. I want my spare keys back, and if you ever come here again I'm going to file a restraining order.

She was hooked. It was only a matter of time before she got off work, so later that night I prepared for her arrival by taking off my clothes and opening a fresh box of Merlot that I was saving for mud wrestling on pay-per-view. I decided to pour myself a few cups of the wine while I was waiting, and I guess I drank too much because the next morning I woke up on the floor and couldn't remember the night of passion we had. I looked around the room and there was broken glass everywhere; she was in such a hurry to hump me rotten that she came through my front window, and accidentally took my wallet, couch, TV, computer, stereo, and VCR along with her spare keys. It was the best sex I ever had.

WHO TO TARGET

The best part of a quickie is that it is, as its namesake implies, quick. So when you're spent thirty seconds after you start, it's not only understandable, it's a requisite. Sex marathons get tiring. You have to stay there, bobbing over her, back and forth, in and out. We get it, enough already. Sex should be simple: get in, get out, and go back to work. Men have shit to do; we don't have time to spend all day bumping uglies. A guy's balls can only take so much friction before we say "fuck it" and stop fucking it.

Though using a seductive tape can help, the key to a really great quickie is spontaneity. One way to be more spontaneous is to walk around all day with your pants down. You never know when you might get lucky.

There are five main types of women that you will be able to score a quickie with:

1. Hot chicks with a positive self-image and strong confidence.
2. Ugly chicks with a positive self-image and strong confidence.
3. Hot chicks with low self-esteem.
4. Ugly chicks with low self-esteem.
5. Fat chicks.

The reason the "fat chick" category above wasn't broken down is because fat chicks are pretty much broken down already. Of the types above, ugly chicks in category #2 are the most annoying, not because they're ugly, but because they think they're not. Ugly chicks with confidence are constantly grappling with identity crisis by thinking that they belong to category #1.

SETTING THE TRAP

Women feel vulnerable after sex, and this is especially true if they get nothing from it (likely). If you want to score a follow-up quickie, you need to take advantage of this fact by lowering her self-esteem. The first time you score with her, you need to make sure to put your best foot forward and impress the hell out of her. Make it quick, but keep it classy. This will bait her into thinking you're a great lover, and she'll be willing to do the three-pump crotch tango with you again at some point.

After sex, you need to plant the seeds of self-doubt into her mind by telling her that she was "pretty good." The word "pretty" used in this context will act as a buffer to lessen the effect of the word "good," causing her to wonder what exactly about her performance caused you to hold back your compliment. If done correctly, her self-esteem will be lowered, giving you a great opportunity for a follow-up quickie, at which time you can be as unspectacular as you want.

The only exception to this rule is when a woman has low self-esteem to begin with. A good way to find out is to make an offhanded comment about her physical appearance or smell, and if she doesn't react with violence, then it's a safe bet that she's insecure. Make her like you on a superficial level by getting her to laugh, and you're set (Figure 1).

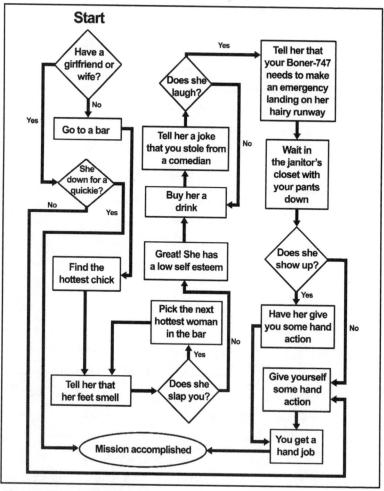

Figure 1: The quickie flowchart.

 is for...
ROAD RAGE

ROAD RAGE IS AN OFF-PUTTTING PHRASE because the word "rage" has negative connotations, invoking thoughts of chaos and anarchy. A more fitting phrase would be "road justice," because in the lawless wasteland known as the interstate highway system, each man must make his own justice, sometimes with the help of a tire iron.

Generally speaking, road rage happens under the following conditions:

> **WHEN YOU ARE ON A ROAD**

REASONS FOR RAGE

Men who experience road rage often have it because it's a well-known fact that road rage makes women horny. One time, I yelled out the window at some guy and my girlfriend got so wet that I dove into her vagina, and not in the metaphorical sense, I mean literally a cannonball into her pussy. It was so wet that I invited all the neighbors in to play a game of marco polo, but not their kids because that would be weird.

Sometimes, when other drivers on the road are too meek to stand up for themselves, you must do it for them. For example, I was driving down a two-lane road one time when I saw in my rearview mirror that all the cars were pulling over to the side because some big-shot asshole was trying to get through. I wasn't about to pull over just because this guy had a tricked out truck with flashing red lights and his name painted on the front. It's one thing when you paint your name on your car because it's cool like "Hernandez," but what kind of name is "KCURT ERIF"?

So there I was, driving down the road when this asshole started tailgating me. I then stuck a hand out the window and made the most obscene gesture I could think of: putting my fist up to my mouth, pushing the side of my cheek with my tongue; it looked like I had a dick in my mouth, suggesting that he should "suck it" (Figure 1).

Figure 1

Then he got really pissed and started honking his horn, which was a lot louder than a normal horn, but was I intimidated? You bet your ass I wasn't. He swerved to the left to go around me, but that only strengthened my resolve, and I cut him off just in time so he'd have to drive behind me over the bridge for the next mile. Then I noticed that he had a Dalmation in the front seat of his truck, so I knew that this guy was loaded.

Since I'm just as tired of being bullied around by these rich fucks as the next guy, I decided to play a little game with him. I waved him over to the side of the road, and he got out of the truck along with a bunch of his buddies. The first thing he said was, "What the fuck is your problem?" So I yelled back, "What the fuck is *your* problem?" with extra emphasis on "your" because I wanted to say "My problem? I don't have a problem pal, you're the one who has the problem" in a way that only emphasizing one word can. He looked super pissed and was about to take a swing at me, so I ducked down, ran between his legs, head-butting his balls as I went through, then I ran up to the window of his truck and threw his dog into the river.

I was laughing so hard I shit myself.

Then, another time, I was driving on the sidewalk and out of nowhere this guy hit my car; even though he broke my windshield, I decided to be nice by giving him a lift home since most of him was in the passenger seat already. I rang the doorbell and asked his wife for a shovel and a bucket to bring him inside. Next thing I know, the crazy bitch started crying and screaming at me, so I backed up my car, drove straight into her living room, and peeled out on her daughter's face. By now she was going ape shit and I wasn't about to take lip from this woman, so I went upstairs, jerked off on her good linens, and left.

ROAD RAGE

THE LANGUAGE OF ROAD RAGE

You may find that you won't always have time to express yourself to other drivers in a meaningful way. For this reason, a set of commonly used gestures and symbols has been developed over time by drivers to facilitate more efficient communication:

- **RAISE THE ROOF:** This is what you do when you're stuck behind some asshole who's blocking the intersection, and you finally get her attention by honking your horn. You know it's futile to honk, but at least you've made eye contact through her rearview mirror. You usually have several seconds before she'll turn away, so quickly raise your arms in the air, and wave them like you're just not concerned. Remember, the emotion you're trying to convey here is anger, so make sure to crease your eyebrows toward the middle of your forehead. This means you're angry.

- **THE LIP-SYNCH:** This is ideal when people cut you off. Simply drive up next to them, look into their window while you slowly shake your head back and forth as if you're saying "no." Be sure to mouth the phrase "motherfucker" so there's no confusion as to your message.

  There are only a handful of four-syllable words in the English language that start with the letter "M" with an "F" sound in the middle, and most drivers will assume that you're not mouthing the word "malfunctioner" in this context. Another effective word to mouth is "asshole" because of the great contrast between the shapes your lips will make while pronouncing each part of the word. Even though the other driver (usually) won't be able to hear you, he'll understand how pissed you are if you have rich enough facial expressions. Spread the wealth.

• **ONE-FINGER SUNROOF SALUTE:** Giving the bird while you're driving has become a formality. When you see another driver giving it to you, it's standard procedure to acknowledge, nod your head, and return the gesture as if to say "Roger that. Fuck you too. Over."

One of the most effective times to implement the finger is when you're being tailgated. Simply launch your fist through the sunroof and blast away. If you want to come across as being an especially big hardass, punch through the sunroof instead of sliding it open.

• **FINGER WAGGING:** Reserved for geriatrics that get upset while driving, but are too pussy to exchange the universal hand signal. People who wag their fingers at you are expressing disapproval on one side of the coin, and their crippling inability to do anything about it on the other. It's best to wave them over to the side of the road, coax them into stepping out of the car, then bullying them into giving you their groceries. Don't let your conscience get in the way; you're doing these people a favor by sculpting them into better people. The world is tough, and if you don't stand up for yourself, I will eat your food.

• **THE DOUBLE DEUCE:** When one barrel just isn't enough, let loose with both arms to let them know you think they're especially big shit stabbers. An unintended side effect of the double deuce is that you will lose complete control of your car, so you'll swerve back and forth wildly for added effect.

HOW TO BE A MORE EFFICIENT ASSHOLE

These communication protocols coupled with one of the following methods will help you become the ultimate asshole on the road:

- **TALK ON YOUR CELL PHONE:** Talking on the phone while you're driving is awesome. It's not only discourteous to the people riding with you but also to the people on the road because you're saying, "I'm not only jeopardizing my life, but yours and your family's too, so I can continue to have small talk while I drive home."

- **TAG TEAM:** If you're in the far right lane of traffic on the freeway, and the guy next to you is trying to merge into your lane so he can exit, don't let him! If he speeds up to pass, you speed up too. If he slows down to come in from behind, you slow down too! If your friend happens to be driving on the freeway with you, try to coordinate the effort with your cell phone to box the person in (Figure 2). By talking on your cell, not letting the person merge, and following through with a double deuce, you can become the ultimate asshole on the road.

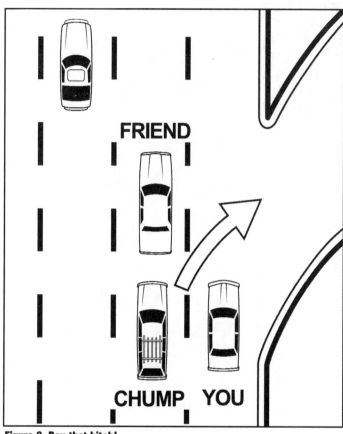

Figure 2: Box that bitch!

 is for...
SNEAKING A PEEK

SNEAKING A PEEK is a distant relative of copping a feel. There's an old proverb that says, "There's no such thing as a free lunch." When you sneak a peek, you not only get a free lunch but you also don't even have to tip. Though calling it lunch is a bit misleading, because lunch is something that can be depleted, whereas the sight of a woman's breasts is not expendable.

Not unlike Mother Theresa, women who wear revealing clothes are humanitarians. While Mother Theresa nourished the hungry, scantily clad women feed the eyes of the horny—or more accurately, the soon to be horny. They're providing a public service to men, women, and children alike in the form of an eye full of copious bosom.

In recent years, feminists have turned the positive act of checking out a nice rack into a negative one that objectifies women. To suggest that women are objectified implies that the subtle glances they receive in public (and occasionally through the lens of binoculars) are unwelcome intrusions. But are they really? To answer this question, one only needs to observe a popular piece of woman's clothing: the v-neck (Figure 1).

Figure 1

The v-neck shirt isn't really a shirt so much as an advertisement. Looking at the shape of a v-neck reveals that the "v" is really an arrow that points straight to a woman's cleavage (Figure 2). This is no accident, and women know this; that's why they wear v-necks to begin with. By wearing this type of shirt, a woman is sending out an invitation, attention to: your eyes. Feminists believe that ogling can be disrespectful to women. However,

Figure 2

the opposite is true: by not looking at a woman's breasts, you're being disrespectful by turning down a kind invitation. Taking a look at a woman's chest is a friendly gesture, a sign that you come in peace (or that you intend to come in peace later—possibly several times).

WHAT TO LOOK FOR

Not all parts of a woman's body are worth scoping out, so I've documented which ones will result in a chubby, and which ones will result in dead wood.

CAMEL TOE

Camel toe is the outline of a vagina caused by thongs or panties that are pulled too tight—and by "too tight," I mean just right. Camel toe makes the world a better place. If there were any justice in this world, politicians would put aside their petty bickering for a few minutes to make it a national law that all women must (a) wear thongs and (b) give themselves wedgies each day. The second law would be optional because it's not necessary for women to give themselves wedgies. I will volunteer.

Camel toe (Figure 3) can usually be spotted at the beach, the gym, and if a woman wears very tight pants (spandex is especially conducive), just about anywhere. Staring at a woman with camel toe is easier than one might expect. Women who sport the toe usually don't realize it. There's

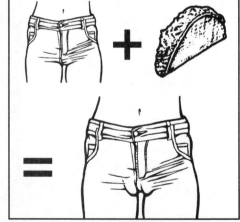

Figure 3: Look for a mound near her panty line. It should look like she has a taco down her pants.

generally no reason for a guy to stare at the crotch area of a woman when she's wearing pants, so glancing between her legs won't set off her perv detectors immediately. Take a look and try to spot a protuberance or a large crease running down the middle.

WHALE TAIL

A whale tail is what happens when a woman's thong naturally hugs the curvature of her hips so that the top of the thong can be seen slightly above the pant line. It's worth giving extra emphasis to the word "naturally" in this definition, because some women try to fake having an ass by pulling their thongs up their backs. As such, finding a good whale tail has become exceedingly difficult.

> • **SPOTTING A FAKE:** Spotting a fake whale tail is easy,
> once you know what the real deal looks like. Its distinc-
> tive look comes from the continuation of the roundness
> of the buttocks through the iliac crest and toward the
> hip (Figure 4).

Figure 4: On the left, we see Captain Ahab's wet dream. As the ass becomes flatter, however, the tail's shape becomes increasingly more level until . . . tragedy

SNEAKING A PEEK

By contrast, a fake tail has flat handles that go around a woman's lower back and could almost double as a belt. It's important not to chastise women who sport the fake tail because these women are suffering from a very serious disorder called "ass identity crisis"— they think they have fine asses when they do not—it's not their fault. These poser asses are an unexpected consequence of the types of jobs women occupy. A more technical term for this condition is "secretary ass."

PLUMBER'S CRACK

A plumber's crack is so potently unsexy that a single drop of it can ruin an entire bathtub full of perfectly good lesbian germs—said to be the most powerful aphrodisiac in the universe. Here are some signs that you've seen plumber's crack:

- •Watery eyes
- •Bad taste in your mouth
- •You stare, but you don't really see
- •Children around you cry for no reason
- •Erectile dysfunction

The problem is that a plumber's crack on a woman is as sexy as a plumber's crack on a man: not. It's just a hint of ass, and the hint is unfortunately not enough to differentiate what you're seeing from a man's ass. Avoid.

PANTIES

Panties have the potential of being the best target to look for while sneaking a peek. The reason is because throughout the course of the day, panties tend to ride, slip, and slide to the side. If you happen to glance at one while she's riding up an escalator, you might get lucky and catch a glimpse of her bearded chalupa.

HOW TO SPOT CLEAVAGE

There are two primary ways to spot cleavage:

1. **THE TOP-DOWN METHOD:** To employ this technique, simply gain the upper ground by getting on a bridge, step ladder, or even on the shoulders of your subject. Women who wear low-cut shirts are perfect for spotting because of the relative ease with which you can view without getting caught. Unless the woman is paranoid, she probably won't look up to see if there's some asshole looking down her shirt. Beware of women with boyfriends, however. Guys know all the techniques employed by perverts like you, so they're always on the lookout for your prying eyes.

2. **THE BEND:** The best opportunity to catch an eye full of a woman's lust pods is when she bends over. Some men speculate that women who do this are usually conscious of their vulnerability, thus allowing men to take a gander. While this is certainly good, it's not "sneaking" a peek in the strictest sense. If a woman lets you browse the goods for free, then you're not seeing anything you're not supposed to, and if you don't have to work to earn it, then it loses some of its value. By all means, be on the lookout for women who bend over with low-cut shirts, but if they don't feel your creepy eyes scanning their bodies after a few seconds, be suspicious.

SNEAKING A PEEK

T is for...
TAUNTING

T **AUNTING IS A REMARK** or action intended to hurt people's feelings or to make them feel upset, angry, or inadequate. Why is taunting manly? Since taunting is, by definition, intended to make people feel bad about themselves, it's an insensitive act. The opposite of insensitive is sensitive, or caring about other's feelings. Women are sensitive, and since men are the opposite of women, men are insensitive by nature. Therefore, taunting is manly.

There needs to be some clarification about what taunting is and isn't. Taunting is not the same as making fun of someone. The main difference is that you can make fun of someone behind his or her back, whereas taunting is done directly to a person's face. Making fun of people behind their back kicks ass. It not only gives you the satisfaction of laughing at people's expense but also helps you be more prepared to make fun of them to their faces, so you don't waste any time trying to think of things to tease them about when you see them. Think of it as training camp for teasers. For example, I make fun of my friends behind their backs all the time. In fact, I have a friend who has a stuttering problem, and I know he'll never read this book; so he's never going to find out that I made fun of his s-s-s-speech impediment in my b-b-b-book.

DEALING WITH CHAMPIONS OF THE MEEK

Critics of taunting claim that people who mock others do it because they have a low self-esteem. The people who try to help victims of taunting have good intentions and tend to view things in a positive light; so rather than writing you off as a "bad seed," they'll try to understand the reason you mock others. This is very valuable because what these empathizers have given you is an excuse for your behavior! Acknowledge it, embrace it, and exploit it to the fullest. If people chastise you for mocking others, feed into their egos and tell them that you have low self-esteem. These self-appointed guardians of the timid love having their theories validated, and telling them exactly what they want to hear will soften them up and get them to bring guards down (Figure 1). Now all you need to do is to make up a reason for your poor self-image. Here are a few good excuses you can use:

Figure 1: Deceive your critics with a sob story to get them to sympathize with you.

TAUNTING

- •Your father is an alcoholic.
- •You grew up in poverty.
- •Your parents were physically abusive.
- •Your parents are going through a divorce.
- •You just got out of an abusive relationship.
- •You were teased as a child.
- •You're coping with the loss of a loved one.
- •You have a learning disorder that makes you feel inferior
  to others.
- •You can't read.
- •You have a bed-wetting problem.

The low self-esteem guise is useful because you're not only excusing your actions, but with the right excuse, you can go so far as to actually gain the sympathy of your victims! To do this effectively, you must feign sincerity by making them believe you truly feel bad for making fun of others. Nothing is more satisfying to a taunting opponent than having the teaser feel remorse for what he has done. Put on a good show and really jerk those tears.

Once you've softened them up, you're ready to strike again. Teasing people after you've gained their trust is especially hurtful to them. They believed your story, they put themselves in your shoes, and they felt bad for your condition. When it dawns on them that they've been manipulated, even the most levelheaded mediators will get pissed off.

HOW TO DEAL WITH THICK SKIN

Counselors often claim that the best way to deal with people who tease you is to ignore them. They think that if teasers don't get a reaction out of you, they'll eventually get bored and go away. Some victims have taken this advice to heart and will seem impossible to crack. However, based on my many years of taunting experience, there's no skin out there so thick that you can't get under it. Everyone has a breaking point, and everyone will eventually crack with enough time and pressure.

You just need to learn how to push the right buttons. For example, if you have an acquaintance who has been unemployed for a long time, and he has made it very clear to you that he still doesn't have a job, you could remind him by asking, "Do you want to grab a coffee on your lunch break? Oh, wait . . . I'm sorry, I didn't mean to bring that up." But you did. The beauty of this strategy is that your question seems innocent, yet it's engineered to make him feel bad. Just find a flaw or a dent in their skin and poke at it. Eventually, that dent will grow into an open wound. Gain their trust, bring them in close, and then rip them a new hole. Being a jerk turns on women. If your friend happens to be a chick, you might even get laid out of it. Women who feel bad about themselves are easy.

WHO TO TAUNT

Choosing a good target for your taunting can be just as important as the content of your jeers. Here are a few disorders and disabilities you can work with.

PEOPLE WHO WEAR GLASSES: It's getting increasingly difficult to tease people who wear glasses because of the popularity and acceptance of children's characters like Harry Potter. By making the protagonists in their books look nerdy, authors like J. K. Rowling have shattered the notion of what a hero should look like, emboldening kids who wear glasses by making them think that they're just as capable, or even as cool as normal kids. So if you choose people who wear glasses, you have to work extra hard to make them feel bad about themselves.

A good starting point is to keep in mind that people who wear glasses have flawed vision. They don't say "perfect 20/20" vision for nothing. Make sure you point that out, and drive the point home by challenging your victim to a reading contest. Just find a sign that's far enough so that your target won't be able to read it, but not so far that you can't read it yourself. Next, tell your target to remove his glasses before reading the sign. If he insists on using his glasses, then suggest that perhaps you should be able to use a visual aid as well—such as a pair of binoculars. After conceding to your bulletproof argument, you should have no trouble reading the sign and proving once and for all that you're normal[1] and your victim is flawed. Don't hesitate to use clichéd nicknames such as "four-eyes" to torment your target. As much as he pretends not to be bothered by it, he'll go home and quietly cry himself to sleep.

PEOPLE WHO WEAR BRACES: The one thing worse than glasses are braces. Braces look nasty. People who wear them have to constantly pick shit out of them, and they need special water picks, floss, brushes, and mouth wash. Anything that requires that much maintenance isn't worth it. I've given up full college scholarships to avoid filling out a few forms, so there's no way in hell I'm going to go through that much trouble, and all for what? A smile? Men don't need to smile. A scowl is good enough.

People who wear braces are narcissistic. They think that others not only care about how they look but also care enough to notice their teeth. The sheer audacity of these oral elitists is mindboggling, and that's why they're great targets for verbal abuse. Let them know that nobody will appreciate their smile years from now when they finally get those atrocious things removed. Act especially disgusted every time you see a brace-wearer show their teeth. This will chisel away at their self-confidence and make you look like a badass.

ANOREXICS: Since most anorexics are always on edge, taunting them requires very little effort or premeditation. For example, if you have an anorexic girlfriend, you can get the job done by simply giving her a shirt that's one size too

1. At least as normal as someone who gains self-satisfaction from taunting people who wear glasses can be.

small, and if she happens to be particularly slow, you might even want to add "... and if it doesn't fit, I can exchange it for a larger size." The great thing about anorexic women is that no matter how skinny they are, they'll always think of themselves as fat.

VEGETARIANS: The problem with vegetarians is that most of them are so pompous about their diets. They go out of their way to make sure everyone knows that they have special requirements. Although some vegetarians keep their diets to themselves, a great majority strain to remind you of what a terrible person you are for eating meat. Of course, to do this, he or usually she must ignore all the animals that are killed as a result of his or her lifestyle in spite of the vegetarian diet. For example, beef tallow is found in virtually every product that exists, from gelatin to paint—even the asphalt you walk on has some cow in it.

This inherent hypocrisy makes vegetarians especially good targets for taunting. Pointing out their ideological inconsistencies is too easy and dignifies their creed much more than it deserves. A better way to taunt them would be to eat as much meat as possible around them. In fact, try to eat not only your share of meat, but their share as well. If you're feeling like a particularly big asshole, you could even eat an extra share of meat to not only nullify their agenda but also to make it worse than if they had never undertaken it to begin with. For every animal that they don't eat, eat three.

ATTENTION DEFICIT DISORDER: Attention deficit disorder (ADD) is a disorder that causes you to have a deficit of attention. Of course, to say that you can have a deficit of attention suggests that you have a finite supply of it, and that there's some fixed amount of attention that is "just right" to have. That means it's not only possible to run out of attention but it's also possible to have an overabundance of it, and yet, there is no such thing as an attention overabundance disorder—at least until a drug can be marketed for this as-of-yet pending epidemic. People who claim to have ADD take

TAUNTING

their illness very seriously, blaming everything from poor test scores to failed relationships on this disorder.

You would think that tearing down this delicate house of cards would be easy—after all, you're dealing with a disease that has no objective criteria for evaluating patients, no quantitative way to measure results, a list of symptoms so vague that it makes the panties of pharmaceutical executives moist, and a multibillion-dollar drug industry pushing its wares on every major network every day of the week. The hardest thing about teasing ADD "sufferers" is that they have a crutch, because people love blaming their shortcomings on outside forces. For example, if you don't have a girlfriend, don't worry; it's not your fault, you have a pussy deficit disorder—a very serious disease that causes your penis to have fewer orgasms. See? Anyone can become a victim!

Though it's difficult to get through to these melodramatic sufferers, it's not impossible. Start by making a strong, confrontational statement such as "ADD doesn't exist." You'll often encounter rebuttals such as "but my mom has it and I got it from my mom." Note that this response doesn't "say" anything since they're just reasserting what they originally claimed. Just keep asking them for proof that they have ADD. It may help to point out that one of the makers of a popular drug[2] that supposedly treats ADD even states on its own Web site that "the precise mechanism by which [the drug] works is not known."

Once you've backed them into the corner, immediately stop and concede to the debate. This may seem counterintuitive, but it's necessary for what comes next: Find their medication and replace all the pills with sugar tablets. After a few weeks of taking sugar pills, confirm that they still feel great, and then break the news to them. They'll be so pissed that their made-up disorder doesn't exist that they'll develop a disease that does: high blood pressure.

2. I won't mention which one, but it rhymes with Strattera.

is for...
URINAL ETIQUETTE

IT NEVER FAILS TO SURPRISE ME when I use a public restroom and find guys who still don't know proper urinal etiquette. This hallowed code of bathroom ethics has been passed down from generation to generation. Yet in spite of this timeless honor code, some men—due to ignorance or malice—choose to break even the most basic of these as-of-yet-unspoken rules. Here's a primer for those of us who are still uninitiated in the ways of the urinal.

RULE #1: DON'T SPEAK UNLESS SPOKEN TO, AND EVEN THEN, DON'T SPEAK

You stand at a urinal for one purpose, and one purpose only: to piss. You should only have one thing coming out of any orifice on your body at any given time; if one hole is open, the other should be closed (Figure 1). Leave the talking to politicians and women (or in some unfortunate circumstances, women politicians). Here's a phrase that will help you remember this rule:

"HOLD YOUR PEACE WHILE YOU HOLD YOUR PIECE."

Talking while conducting your business at a john is unbecoming of a man. A rule of thumb is to not utter one syllable from the second when the stream starts, until the moment the last drop falls.[1] If you don't see an obvious problem with talking while going to the bathroom, here's an elaboration of a few of the possible topics you could discuss, and the problem with each.

TOPIC	WHY YOU SHOULDN'T TALK ABOUT IT
Children	So you're holding your penis, standing next to a guy who's also holding his penis, talking about kids. I'll just say this much: If I'm ever standing next to a guy in a public restroom while he's talking about children, I'm calling the police.
Work	What's so pressing about your job that you have to talk about it while taking a leak? It's hardly conversation-worthy when you're not standing at a urinal, so what makes you think anyone wants to hear about it with his dick out?
Wife	Nobody cares.
Sex Life	Talking about your sex life while at a urinal might cause someone to wonder why you were reminded of sex while taking a leak in the first place. Unless you feel comfortable outing yourself as somebody who enjoys being pissed on for sexual gratification, avoid it. Nobody wants to know what gets you off, especially if it involves another person squatting over your mouth.
Small talk/i.e. "How's it hanging?"	Anyone who asks "how's it hanging" doesn't really want to know how "it's" hanging, otherwise he could simply take a peek.

1. The exact moment this happens is a contentious issue among contemporary scholars. Some believe the last drop that lands in the bowl is the end of the event, while others believe that no matter how much you shake it and bang it against the stall, the last drop won't fall until you put it in your pants.

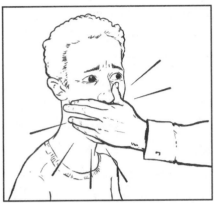

Figure 1: Hey, did you hear the one about the guy who wouldn't shut up while he was taking a leak? I heard he got his ass kicked.

RULE #2:
NO PEEKING

Under no circumstance should one ever peek at another guy's unit while using a urinal. Think of it as visual kryptonite. Just don't do it— I've seen friendships ruined over this. If you happen to catch a glimpse of your friend while he's doing the deed, there's nothing to talk about; just pick up your shit and go. Here's another useful phrase to help you remember this important rule:

"DON'T GAWK AT THE COCK."

You may be thinking "what's the big deal, it's just a penis, grow up!" No. You grow up. Think about it: You're filling your eyes full of photons that have bounced off another man's penis. Those photons carry with them some amount of cock. You wouldn't fill your eyes full of eye drops that had been bounced off another man's dick, so why make an exception for quantum packets of light? (see Figure 2, next page)

After the initial feeling of anger and confusion subside, a subject who has witnessed the penis of another man standing at a urinal will soon experience the onset of disenchantment with life. Things that once tasted good will taste bitter, video games will start to suck, and he will eventually develop a taste for women's literature.

I can think of few things I'd like having in my eyes less than a visual of some guy's shaft. In fact, a short list of these things follows:

URINAL ETIQUETTE

- •Battery acid
- •Trapeze artists
- •A microphone
- •Rabbit droppings
- •Two turntables
- •Pink eye
- •Bath water
- •Nail filings
- •Red eye

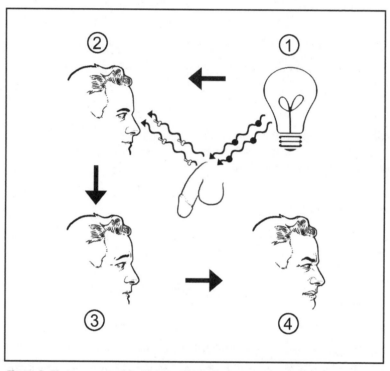

Figure 2: Photons are emitted from a light source (1) and reflect off the surface of the penis, losing some energy in the process and becoming hadrons—a delightfully penile sounding moniker for a subatomic particle—that then travel toward the subject's visual receptor (2). The subject's initial reaction is a feeling of violation (3) followed by intense anger (4).

RULE #3: NO TOUCHING

Don't ever touch anything or anyone in a restroom. This includes—but isn't limited to—combs, newspapers, brushes, stalls, door handles, towel dispensers, towels, faucets, washbasins, toilet seats, flush handles, money clips, soap, and money. Money is especially important to note because it's typically the most tempting of the items mentioned for people to touch. But what if the amount is enough to warrant the risk?

THE $1 RULE

The only exception to the no-touching rule is if you happen to come across currency that is greater than or equal to one U.S. dollar.[2] If you happen upon this bounty, it's fair game to pick it up as long as you don't touch it. There are several techniques for accomplishing this, but the most common is the shirt-sleeve method (Figure 3). Using this method, you are allowed to use the sleeve of your shirt to pick up the bill, but you are strictly prohibited from putting this bill in your pocket. You must take the money and spend it immediately in the first video arcade or vending machine you come across. It's also acceptable to trade this bill with an unsuspecting friend for a noncontaminated bill (or even for lesser money, depending on the discoloration of your bill—use your judgment). If your friend is about to eat something without washing his hands after coming in contact with your shit-bill, you are obligated to suggest that he wash his hands first. Or just snicker quietly.

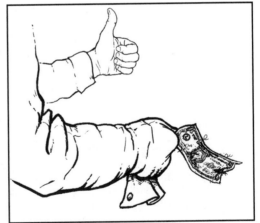

Figure 3: The shirt-sleeve technique will shield you from an array of sexually transmitted diseases commonly found on certain objects in a men's restroom (i.e., everything).

---

2. Or $8 Canadian—since even though the exchange rate isn't that low, it's still Canadian currency, which is perceived as being intrinsically less valuable than all other currencies, Turkey's lira not withstanding.

THE CONTEST

Once you have these rules down, you can relax a little. One of the best things about standing up to pee is that you can aim your stream in an irregular fashion onto various objects. Sadly, there's not much for you to piss on at an ordinary urinal, except the urinal cake. While it gives you something to aim for, it's not much of a challenge—unless you happen to have a pube crossing your gap, in which case the stream might be split and you piss all over yourself like an idiot. Some urinal pads have an antidrug message on them, and these are especially amusing to pee on, because how seriously do you take a message that you piss on to begin with? It's hard to say "no" to drugs when I'm spraying the mandate with my golden shower.

Occasionally, if all the urinal stalls are occupied (more on this later), you may have to use the toilet to take a leak. The toilet can offer a greater number of targets for you to pee on and is often preferable to the urinal for that reason. This is where all your training comes into play, and your skills are tested to their full extent (see Figure 4, opposite).

TARGETS

There are six different categories of targets for you to pee on. Which ones are available to you will usually depend on how seedy the restroom is. Here is a breakdown on which targets you'll find, and the point value to award yourself if you're keeping score.

(A) GRAFFITI, 5 POINTS: Peeing on graffiti is mostly reserved for beginners. The only skill involved is aiming a little higher than usual, and occasionally extending your reach—but this takes minimal effort and can be accomplished with a bit of compression and heaving. The only redeeming quality that comes from pissing on this target is that the person who made the graffiti might eventually return to add more to his work, at which time

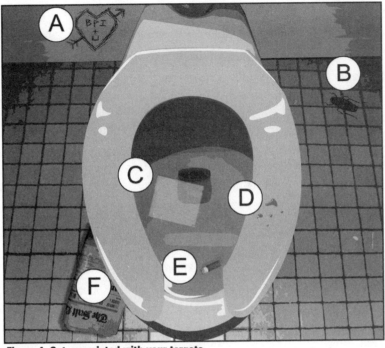

Figure 4: Get acquainted with your targets.

you can take solace in the fact that this budding young artist will be scrawling in the medium of your piss. Be careful not to do this in New York, lest every art snob within a three-mile radius flock around you to discuss amorphous art techniques like "psychic automatism," which is some hardcore bullshit.

(B) INSECTS, 200–1000 POINTS: Perhaps the most challenging object to pee on is an insect. It depends on which kind naturally, but most winged insects are reserved for piss masters. For example, a typical 6-legged insect will easily land you a beefy cache of points in the three-digit realm. The swifter the insect, the more points you get. A cockroach, centipede, or spider, for instance, will get you 200 points. The holy grail of insect targets is a fly, weighing in at a hefty 1,000 points. Flies—much like new-agers—lack purpose in their lives, so they zip around the room arbitrarily to confuse and annoy you. Their erratic flight patterns make them damn near impossible to connect with. If aiming for the fly becomes too frustrating, you can focus your efforts on other flying insects, such as ladybugs. Hitting a ladybug will automatically give you an extra 50 points because women and children are especially fond of these meek creatures.

(C) DRIFTING TOILET PAPER, 15–50 POINTS: Toilet paper is another good introductory water target. There's a large surface area, so it's easy to hit for target practice. Try to aim for the center to tear a hole through it. Sinking a piece will give you 20 points, whereas a hit will give you a mere 15. It's important to note that each subsequent piece of toilet paper beyond the first will give you 5 fewer points than the square before it. However, splitting a chain of toilet paper into smaller squares, then sinking those squares will give you full credit for each piece. On the other hand, if you're able to sink a square down the toilet hole, you may earn up to 50 points for this move.

(D) TOILET SEAT, -5 POINTS: Strictly an amateur move, pissing on the toilet seat is generally looked down upon. Not because you're being a really big douche to the next guy who needs to take a shit, but because it surrounds nearly the entire circumference of the bowl; it's almost harder to miss the toilet seat than it is to hit it. Getting points for pissing on the toilet seat would be like getting points for fucking the Grand Canyon. You can't miss, so there's no challenge, and no challenge = negative points.

(E) CIGARETTE BUTT, 25–100 POINTS: One of the more skill-taxing targets is the butt of a cigarette. Not only is it a small floating target but it is also particularly difficult to sink because of its dense composition of meshed fiber. Using the direct approach, only the most caustic streams will be able to fray the filter enough to tank this target. Your best bet is at a rest stop after a long trip. You need to have several pints in reserve to even be considered a contender.

An alternate strategy is to go for combo points by dipping the butt with your stream, then trying to maneuver it underneath a drifting square of toilet paper (Figure 5). While the butt technically hasn't touched the bottom of the bowl, it's still submerged under water, and it will only be a matter of time before it becomes so waterlogged that it sinks (Figure 6). This is an advanced strategy, and successful implementation will score you 100 points for technique, plus you get bragging rights. Your peers may have difficulty believing you—and rightfully so—so you

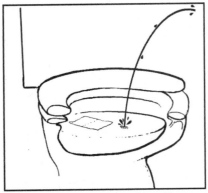

Figure 5: Striking the butt with a direct hit and correct stream orientation will force the butt underneath a square of toilet paper.

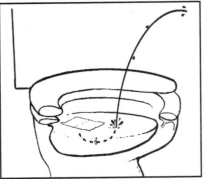

Figure 6: Success! Within minutes your target will sink, garnering the praise of all who come within earshot of your bragging mouth.

URINAL ETIQUETTE

may need to take pictures or get a witness to vouch for your accomplishment. Note: mothers and girlfriends aren't as impressed by this achievement as your buddies will be, so use them as a last resort.

(F) NEWSPAPERS, 10–20 POINTS: The satisfaction of peeing on a newspaper comes from the potential for some unsuspecting patron to touch it after you've soiled it with your misdeed. The obvious approach would be to piss directly on the newspaper, but this is stupid because peeing on paper will cause it to wrinkle when it dries. So you're faced with a dilemma: how can you soak the newspaper without making it look obvious? Simple: piss all over the place around it. You can cake the paper with tiny sprinkles of urine that go unnoticed to those who lack a critical eye. The other difficulty with pissing around a newspaper comes from the sprinkles that miss your target. These piss particles can and will coat everything they come in contact with, including your shoes, clothing, and if you're unfortunate enough to wear shorts while trying to pull off this maneuver, your shins. Since the payoff is so low, many choose to forego this object in favor of more rewarding targets. Pissing directly onto the newspaper without getting any on you will score 10 points, while a perfect execution using the sprinkle method can garner up to 20.

THE ORDER

This may come as a surprise to some, but which urinal a man chooses when he goes into a restroom makes a world of difference. It's a well-known fact that using a urinal next to another man when you don't absolutely need to means you want to have sex with him. If this isn't your intention, then you must heed the order of the piss priority when you use a john. For example, if a restroom has four stalls and you're the only person inside the restroom, you must choose the stall furthest from the entrance, next to a wall if possible, giving priority to urinals before toilets; this is stall A. The next man must then choose the next available urinal, keeping one stall in separation between you two at all times, which would be stall C. If a third man comes into the restroom while the other two are going, he must wait until stall A or stall C is no longer in use before he can go, unless it's a dire emergency, and even then your peers are allowed to assume that you wish to partake in anal sex with another man.

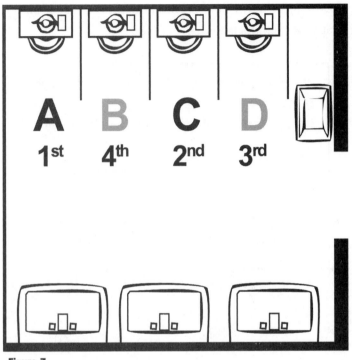

Figure 7

In a worst-case scenario—one in which you are forced to use a urinal next to one that is already occupied—you should always choose stall D before stall B to minimize the number of consecutive wangs (Figure 7).

Although the four-stall configuration is the one you'll encounter most, a more general approach is necessary when using mega rest-rooms in stadiums, casinos, and internment camps. For example, when using a restroom with ten stalls and five patrons, the first person should use stall A next to the wall, like in the four-stall scenario. The next person should use the third stall, the third person should use the fifth stall, and so on. Memorizing this priority queue can be useful, but becomes rather cumbersome as the number of stalls grows larger. A more convenient way to sort out this problem is to use a simple formula derived from the following sequence:

> *In general, if we take s to be the number of stalls, and n to be the number of patrons, you can find out which stall you should use with the following simple equation:*
>
> **Stallposition** $= n+(n-1)$
> $= 2n-1$ **where n < s/2**

For example, if you're the 5th patron and there are 10 stalls, the equation yields 2(5) - 1 = 9, so you'd use the 9th stall (Figure 8).

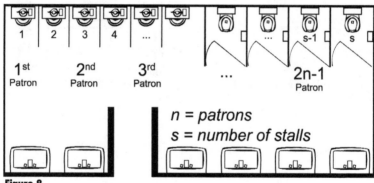

Figure 8

is for...
VIOLENCE

EVER WONDER WHY EVERY TIME an archeologist discovers a new fossil of ancient man, it's always a piece of his jawbone or a fragment of his wrist? The reason you rarely find a whole skeleton intact isn't because of weathering, erosion, or any of the other theories that ivory tower intellectuals are always trying to shove down our throats. It's because men love violence, and every red-blooded man wants to die as violently as possible. In fact,

Figure 1: Holy shit!

man's very existence depends on it; without finding increasingly more violent ways to end life, the romantic comedy industry would slowly whittle away at the fabric of man's being until all that's left is an overly sensitive eunuch who cries himself to sleep. Violence builds character. Why settle for sucking on modern medicine's teat as you rot away in a retirement home when you can stand up on a roller coaster and have every bone in your face smashed in a spectacular display of regulatory defiance (Figure 1)?

OH NO! NOT ANOTHER BORING OBITUARY!

"Passed away peacefully" are three of the worst words you can read in an obituary. Only pussies pass away; men are choked, drowned, stabbed, and pushed into wood chippers (sometimes simultaneously). Take my grandpa for example: While serving in Vietnam, he was captured behind enemy lines, tortured for weeks, had both legs amputated, and finally he was strapped to a land mine and drop kicked into a village full of angry Vietcong who taunted him by dangling their genitals in his face (Figure 2). Naturally, he lived to tell the story, and many years later when he was about to die, he insisted on having his nurse body slam him through a concrete barrier. Now there was a real man.

Figure 2: My grandpa getting drop kicked into a Vietnamese village.

We've established that men end life as violently as possible, but people pay less attention to the fact that life begins violently as well.

People who oppose violence find it convenient to ignore the fact that violence surrounds every facet of our lives from the earliest stages of conception. Observe:

STAGE 1: INTERCOURSE

Humans procreate through sexual reproduction, and one of the more commonly used phrases to describe this act is "pounding the pussy" or "hitting it." The definition of the word "pounding" is: "to deliver heavy blows repeatedly." A man uses his penis like a fleshy one-eyed battering ram to pound at the gates of a woman's bearded birth canal (Figure 3).

STAGE 2: FERTILIZATION

Once a woman's stronghold has been breached, a flood of sperm will swim through her cervix and across the fallopian tube toward her egg. Sperm are

Figure 3

VIOLENCE

cranky by nature. They spend their lives inside a guy's balls. It's hot, humid, and it stinks in there. They get tired of hanging around nuts all day, so when a man ejaculates, they get excited at the prospect of freedom.

Even after they escape, a sperm's survival is a long shot because a great number of them will perish upon a crumpled wad of tissue like so many others before them. It's the hope of one day getting shot by a guy who's not a loser that keeps them going. So when they finally enter a vagina for the first time, the sperms are understandably anxious. They will shove, maim, and kill to get to the finish line (Figure 4).

STAGE 3: BIRTH

After the sperm champion enters the egg, he is christened as king of sperms, as the rest of the contenders glare on bitterly with equal parts of contempt and sadness. The losers will spend the rest of their lives bumming around the uterus, telling tales of how they "almost went pro," until they wither away depressed and forgotten.

Figure 4: A sperm's only chance at becoming somebody.

The king of sperms, exhausted from all the fighting and shit ruining, will then take a break to recoup until the third trimester. During this time, the king will grow into a fetus and will have developed the rudimentary motor skills to kick his mother. These skills will come into use when he gets tired of hearing his mother ramble on about him to her friends and family, and busts his mother right in the craw as a way of saying "Shut it, woman."

Once the child is ready for birth, the baby will force its way through a hole the size of the "O" at the beginning of this sentence. There will be blood. There will be screaming. And there will be lots of tearing. It will mark the end of one violent beginning, and the start of another—life.

VIOLENCE ON A BUDGET

Though violence is a necessary part of life, not all forms of violence are equal. Some means to an end are more expensive than others; choose a method that fits your budget requirements.

Electric Chair: $52

What you need:
- High-quality electrodes $48
- Vegetable strainer $4

Man invented the electric chair as a way of coping with boring dinner guests and disobedient children. Children are ideal candidates for electrocutions because kids are so gullible. One time, I dared a kid to touch an electric fence for five bucks. To my surprise, he took me up on my offer, and I am now five dollars poorer because of it. Just kidding.[1]

Simply attach one electrode to the subject's head, the other to his leg,

1. I didn't pay him.

and connect the lines to an AC power source. The vegetable strainer doesn't really serve any purpose other than to make the subject look ridiculous (Figure 5), but it adds to the atmosphere and gets you in the mood to execute. The reason a chair wasn't included in the cost of this device is because it only serves as a seat and seats can be found

Figure 5

anywhere. A sofa or a stool could be used just as easily. The only reason you have to use a chair is because the name "electric chair" would be just "electric" without it, which sounds stupid.

SNEEZE IN SOMEONE'S FACE: $0

WHAT YOU NEED:

•Lungs $0
•Communicable disease $0

I know, you're probably thinking, "But Maddox, lungs are priceless!" Get a life, seriously. As for the communicable disease, anything such as malaria, botulism, or dysentery will work. Botulism is an unconventional choice because it's usually spread by eating contaminated food that has not been properly cooked or canned; it does not spread by physical contact. To spread botulism, you have to get a mouth full of uncooked meat, then run up to your subject, hold his nose shut, and when he opens his mouth to breathe, sneeze in it.

As for dysentery, transmission usually occurs by coming into contact with doorknobs, silverware, or food infected with shit particles spread by assholes who don't wash their hands after taking a dump. While the transmission of dysentery isn't violent, the result is severe projectile diarrhea that will demolish the subject's ass.

MAGNIFYING GLASS HAT: $38.55

WHAT YOU NEED:

- Magnifying glass $30
- Metal strip $7
- Popsicle sticks $0.75
- Scotch tape $0.80

Simply affix the lens to the metal strip using Popsicle sticks (Figure 6), and put the hat on. If set at the correct height (about 3" or 8 cm), you should feel an intense pain at the top of your head as the sun burns a hole through your skull and

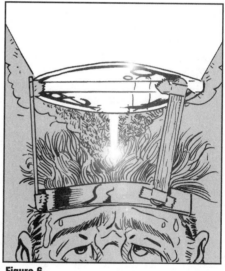

Figure 6

brain tissue. This method only works on a sunny day, so wait until the weather is good to kill yourself.

SMOTHERING SOMEONE TO DEATH WITH A PLACENTA: $12.95

WHAT YOU NEED:

- Placenta $12.95

I don't really know how much a placenta costs, but you can buy a lamb placenta for $12.95 and I figure that a human placenta probably doesn't cost much more. And if it does, you're probably getting ripped off.

When you smother someone to death with a placenta, you're using the beginning of someone's life as a means to end someone's life. The smothering doesn't actually kill the victim, but rather, his head will explode because of the sheer irony.

WOOD CHIPPER: $0

WHAT YOU NEED:
- •Wood chipper $2500
- •Hippies   -$2500

Hippies cost a negative amount of money, so in other words people would have to pay you to take them. Wood chippers are great not only because they're violent but also because they piss off environmentalists in the following ways:

1. Wood chippers can shred trees.

2. Wood chippers can shred environmentalists.

When selecting a wood chipper, there are several features you may want to look for, such as power feed and reversible blades for those times when you're clearing your property of activists and your wood chipper gets jammed (Figure 7).

Figure 7

 **is for...**
WINNER

A **WINNER IS A LOSER WHO SUCKS AT LOSING**, and if there's anything I suck at, it's losing.

Here's the definitive list of winners:
- Me
- King Ghidorah
- Steve Buscemi
- Lesbians
- Flying squirrels
- Red Twizzlers
- Castlevania: 1, 3, 4, Symphony of the Night, Dawn of Sorrow

- Kung Pao shrimp
- Theodore Roosevelt
- Moshi Moshi
- Ivan the Terrible
- Extra sharp cheddar cheese
- Monsters
- Fried chicken
- Chops

HOW TO WIN

People often ask me, "Maddox, you're handsome, smart, witty, successful, testicularly blessed, and you smell really good, like smoked ham. How do you do it? How does one person become such a spectacular winner?" Here's how:

RULE #1:
ALWAYS COMPETE WITH WEAKER OPPONENTS

Specifically: animals, children, old people, and mental patients.

I have a friend who's sixty-eight and has dementia, and there's nobody I'd rather play chess with. That's because sometimes he forgets where he is or what game we're playing, so I can take my time to rearrange the pieces on the board. When it's his turn, he looks distressed and confused and sometimes pulls his hair out. My girlfriend was scornful when she found out why I was so gleeful every time I came back from the retirement home. She said, "I bet you feel pretty good about yourself by picking on an old man." Yeah, it felt great. We broke up shortly after. Win/win.

Another example is when my siblings came over last year for Thanksgiving, and the conversation at the time mostly revolved around how much my seven-year-old nephew had grown since the last time everyone saw him. I could tell that he was getting cocky about it. Each new compliment went straight to his head, fueling his ego. So I finally got fed up and said, "Think you're so big? How about we try to scare each other to see who wins?" He accepted my challenge and his effort culminated with him jumping out from behind a plant and yelling "boo" several hours later. I was not impressed. He asked me when I was going to try to scare him, and I told him to fucking wait.

Later that night when everyone was sleeping, I put on an old Moses mask from last Halloween, kicked his door open, and ran in with an electric handsaw. He jumped out of bed screaming and crying and knocked over the lamp on the nightstand. Just as he wet himself, the saw came unplugged and I took the mask off. I said, "I guess I'm bigger after all."

Although competing against kids or the mentally ill is a great way to feel like a winner, it's better to compete against an opponent who is even stupider. For example, I went to the zoo one time and saw a really old chimpanzee drooling in the corner of his cage, so I asked him if he wanted to play the poking game. "The rules are simple," I explained. "I try to poke you with a stick, and if I miss, it's your turn to try to poke me. If you want to play, stay quiet." He didn't reply, so I went ahead and poked him. I didn't miss, so I poked him again. He kept howling and jumping up and down until some guards kicked me out. I went home and had a steak to celebrate my victory.

RULE #2:
HANG OUT WITH LOSERS

Hanging out with losers is a great way to make yourself feel like a winner, much in the same way fat people feel skinnier when they hang out with fatter people. Sure, hanging out with losers has its disadvantages; they'll drone on about their problems to you, hit you up for cash, and they smell, but being better than someone at something will make you feel like a relative winner.

WINNER

The superiority you enjoy by having losers as friends needs to be more substantive than just having the relative status. You need to act the part and become a bully by bossing them around and mocking them so you'll be known as the "chief" of the losers. For example, if you make friends with a bunch of anime nerds, you need to be threatening and impose your opinions forcefully during debates about the merits of tentacle cock Hentai. Or if you make friends with a group of boring yuppies, woo them by dropping the names of famous celebrities you've met at restaurants. If you really want to go the extra mile, buy an entry-level luxury car that you can't afford and go out of your way to keep it safe from scratches and bumps by parking at the far end of the parking lot, just like rich people do.

RULE #3:
REDEFINE SUCCESS

When you try your best to do something but just can't succeed, nobody can blame you for not trying. However, for all those times when you dick around and make a half-assed effort, redefining success is sometimes the only way to win. How you define success will determine whether or not you will be a winner.

For example, I technically dropped out of college because I didn't pass a test that would have allowed me to graduate. I had all the other requirements to pass, except for literally one test. But did I fail? Hell no. I've defined success in college as the realization that a degree is a shallow form of self-validation that motivated people don't need to be successful. Want proof? You spent $15.95 on a book written by a college dropout.

WINNER

is for...
X X X

XX IS A SYMBOL adopted by the adult film industry to indicate only the highest-quality pornography is contained within packages with this marking. Pornography is a tool used to facilitate a man's goal to drain his pole. Tugging one's python, as rudimentary as it may seem, is a skill that is a crucial prerequisite to intercourse. Like all skills, if you don't use it enough, you become rusty at it. If you become rusty at it, then you won't be able to procreate, and without procreation, the human race will cease to exist. Therefore, pornography is essential to the survival of mankind.

Since pornography is critical to the continuation of humanity, it's worth mastering the techniques for efficient porn viewing.

The fly in the ointment of any straight porn is the penis. Few things can bum your wood as quickly as the sight of some guy's beef mast stinking up an otherwise perfectly good love scene. Fortunately, there's a time-tested method for circumventing any unwanted cock (excuse the redundancy).

THE THUMB TRICK

The principle behind the thumb trick is simple: close one of your eyes, then put your thumb in front of the eye that remains open. Move the thumb away from your face if the porn star has a small penis, and toward your face if he has a larger one. One of the great things about this cock-dodging technique is the flexibility of it. No matter what angle or position the porn star takes, you can always arrange your thumb to cover the majority of the offending dong (Figures 1–2).

The best way to learn is through experimentation, but as a rule of thumb, the distance you hold your finger away from your eye is

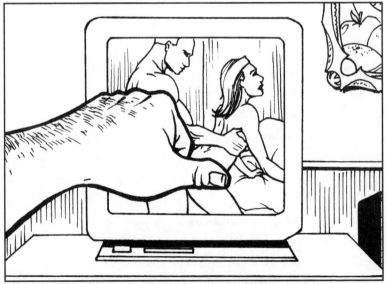

Figure 1: Using the thumb trick with a horizontal orientation to block the cock.

proportional to the screen area displaced by the shaft, the viewable screen size, and the distance you sit away from the screen. For example, if the penis takes up the full width of a seventeen-inch monitor, and you're sitting three feet away from the screen, you would need to hold your thumb nine inches from your face for an effective blocking of the cock (Figure 3).

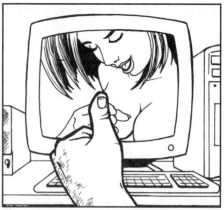

Figure 2: The thumb trick employed here vertically to demonstrate the flexibility of this method.

Figure 3: Sitting three feet away from a seventeen-inch screen, you must hold your thumb nine inches away from your face to effectively block a full-screen cock shot. Note that if the penis remains on the screen for more than five seconds consecutively, you might not be watching straight porn. Then again, you might not be straight, in which case you may proceed.

STEALTH WANKING

ALT + TAB

Here's a tip that will help you avoid getting busted when you watch porn on a computer using Microsoft Windows: press alt + tab to quickly switch your current window to the previous window you had open. You can use the alt + tab method to conceal your porn from snoopy co-workers who peer into your cubicle as they walk by. Now, the only thing left to do is hack into the Web server and filter out your IP address from the access log and you're set.

THE RECALL BUTTON

Let's say you're watching some porn on TV and your parents or your girlfriend are in the room next to you. What do you do if they suddenly come into your room? The most important rule to remember is: don't panic. If you panic, you'll be more likely to stand up, and if you're sporting wood, you're busted. Instead, use the recall button on your remote control (also called "last," "swap," or "memory"). This button will swap the channel you're currently watching with the channel you were last watching. Make sure that the channel you swap to isn't worse than the channel you were watching before; for example, getting caught watching "Animal Planet" with your pants down may be undesirable.[1]

AMASSING YOUR COLLECTION

The path to becoming a porn master is a long and hard one that will take many years and many rolls of toilet paper to conquer. The difficulties in acquiring porn change at different points in a man's life. Here are a few pointers and pitfalls that will aid every man in acquiring a substantial spank bank to withdraw funds from in the currency of filth.

1. Outside Kansas.

ADOLESCENCE: Some of the most difficult challenges in acquiring illicit material will come at the cusp of adolescence when a boy's age will be the determining factor in whether he will play the fiddle with an ensemble, or he'll be hunched over a Sears catalogue, using a middle-aged woman wearing an afghan and khakis for spank fodder.

Most smut is banned from minors because of the irreparable harm it causes to them. You may be wondering what kind of harm it causes, or even if evidence of this harm exists. Suffice it to say that there is a lot of evidence linking teenagers who view pornography with a wide array of harmful conditions such as sex addiction, rape, serial homicide, money laundering, tax evasion, obesity, poor grades, narcolepsy, goiters, neuromuscular joint disorder, impotence, acne, Indian tick fever, and bad breath. Scientists haven't even begun to scratch the surface of all the negative side effects caused by pornography, but there exists mountains of research on it, so that's that.

Luckily, there is a way around the filter if you're old enough to charm your cobra and you have a little cash. The first method involves exploiting the homeless. You can find piles of bums lying around in parks and bus stops and underneath bridges in big cities. Bums are great to employ because they'll work cheap, and they don't ask questions. Just find a bum who's sober enough to walk, and tell him you want some porn. Be sure to make an intimidating threat, like you will cut him if he gets you some crappy all-anal gangbang bullshit.

Once you've found a hapless hobo to take advantage of, give him the money for the porn, and an additional 50 percent of the cost for him to keep. Then tell him that you'll give him an additional 50 percent once he delivers. Homeless people can't be trusted with anything; that's why they're homeless to begin with. So make sure to stare him down—to make it clear that you don't approve of him or his kind; you may even want to hold your nose and breathe to the side while you talk to him. That way the bum will feel bad about himself and he'll be less likely to take advantage of your good nature if he feels downtrodden and depressed—and as every bum knows, depression is nothing a shot of vodka can't lick.

After he gives you the porn, you have a choice to make: you can hold your end of the bargain and pay the bum, or point out that he's contributing to the delinquency of a minor by selling you adult material and threaten to turn him in. The only problem with the latter choice is that the bum might call your bluff, in which case you'll have to give up your porn to the fuzz as evidence to get the bum arrested. The best option here is to find a middle ground by paying him only half of what you promised him: 25 percent, and throw in a half eaten sandwich or a used sock to seal the deal.

EARLY TWENTIES TO EARLY THIRTIES: The twenties are the golden years of wanking. You're finally legal, you have almost a decade of practice with getting in touch with yourself, and unless you're a parasite, you've probably moved out and gone to college by now.

A wonderful new tool called the Internet is now at your disposal. Your first foray into online depravity will be a good, albeit overwhelming, experience. There's so much porn online that you may need zinc supplements to replenish your body of vital nutrients, just so you don't die from your new hobby.

After spending some time with your new arsenal of explicit media, you'll start to notice something: most porn on the Internet sucks. It's hard to find anything "normal" anymore. Dr. Alfred C. Kinsey, a sex researcher who made a splash in academic circles in the '40s, held the position that there is no such thing as "normal sex." After spending some time looking at smut on the Internet, say anywhere from five to ten seconds, it's safe to conclude that Dr. Kinsey was decidedly wrong.

Between all the extreme fisting, foot jobs, bukkake, chubby chick clamp torture, gag sex, bizarre wax torture slaves, circus freaks, balloon animal phallus, piss fetish, spit swapping, strange insertions, femdom mistresses, face sitting, and barf cocks, there's not much room for the type of porn most of us grew up on—the plain old-fashioned kind where it was just a guy and some chick, or just a chick and some chicks.

No matter how unusual and bizarre a fetish is, you'll find people trying to put themselves above others who might have an even weirder, but just as nasty fetish. For example, you'll find that people who are into golden showers claim to enjoy piss porn, but not gargling, as if people who like being pissed on are well adjusted and normal, whereas people who like gargling are nasty and less than human.

I don't know when exactly gaping assholes and double-fisted extreme insertion porn became the norm on the Internet, but it needs to stop. Please. All this ultra raunchy crap will tarnish an otherwise good decade of stroking the tube steak.

After many fruitless nights searching for porn that doesn't suck, you'll find that it may be easier to stick to more conventional smut: magazines and videos, which will take you into the next era.

MID-THIRTIES TO LATE FORTIES: happy times are over. By now, you're probably married or in a long-term relationship. Most women are insecure about themselves and can't stand the idea of a guy enjoying anything that doesn't directly involve them. Women expect men to think about their wives and girlfriends when they have sex, and especially when they don't have sex.

The reason women don't like the idea of men watching porn during relationships is because women feel like they have to compete with porn, when in fact, there's no competition. Porn always wins. Porn doesn't complain about her co-workers asking why she's walking with a limp the next day, it doesn't cry if you lose your balance and knock over her stupid alarm clock (what kind of grown woman has a Hello Kitty alarm clock anyway?) and it doesn't get pissy like a woman does when you tell her to use the payphone down the street to call for a cab after sex.

Having the old battle-axe around the house won't afford you much time to answer the bone-a-phone, let alone use the computer to help you rub one off since it's probably shared. Porn sites have a tendency to fill your computer up with as much evidence of your activities as possible, so you'll find yourself turning to your roots by hiding a few snippets of porn from magazines and videos around your house.

Ironically, one of the better places to hide your porn is inside your computer case. The very computer that you can no longer use to look at porn will now aid you in hiding it from your wife. Women are generally intimidated by technology and will have no reason to ever check inside your computer case—most don't even know that the case can be opened. You can hide your stash in there for years without worrying about the old hag finding out (Figure 4).

A great place to hide your porn is in plain sight, and the increasing popularity of adult DVDs has made it easy to do just that. One of the most overlooked resources in concealing your stash is inside the CD cases you have lying around the house. Simply find a CD that you know your woman won't listen to (see Metal), and then double up your porn underneath the

Figure 4: She'll never suspect a thing.

CD. Make sure to throw away all your DVD cases, or if you have a kid, leave them around in his room so that he takes the heat. With a bit of ingenuity, you can conceal your smut oasis while your significant other continues to slowly crush your spirit.

FIFTIES AND BEYOND: at this stage of the game, most men will have long since conceded to exhaustion of age and family responsibilities in the Wank War. Going through all the trouble of hiding and retrieving porn, then actually having to do the work involved will prove to be too tiring for many. But for the few who plan to keep their turkeys basted 'til the very end, there will be a new challenge to overcome: trying to stay alive.

Since jerking geriatrics are prone to dying of heart attacks, your hobby will become a life-threatening one. While it may make for some interesting conversations at your wake, being caught dead in the act may sully an otherwise perfect stealth-wanking career. Why blemish your record now? Fortunately, there is a way to conceal your activities even in this worst-case scenario.

As you get older, more and more of your porn will come from traditional sources, such as cable and satellite television. Most modern receivers have a feature that allows you to set a timer that will automatically change the channel you're watching to something else. This way if you happen to die while pounding your pole, your horrified grandchildren can't assume the worst when they find your gnarled hand down your pants.

XXX

is for...
YELLING

Y **ELLING IS A UNIVERSAL LANGUAGE.** It doesn't matter what you yell, people always understand the same thing: some shit is going down and they need to get out of the way and possibly call security. Yelling is awesome. I yell all the time, especially when I don't have to. In fact, sometimes it's rude not to yell. For example, I was talking to some chick at a party when all of a sudden she leaned over and whispered into my ear. I could tell the people around me were curious, and I don't blame them because after all, she could be talking behind their backs, as hot women at parties tend to do. So I yelled back, "Right now, in front of all these people? Or did you mean later, like at a hotel?" She tried to slap me, but I ducked and she knocked over a very expensive vase. Then I let her give me a hand job and I walked away.

Sometimes you need to yell in place of irresponsible parents not doing their job. For example, if you see a child mouthing off in public and the parents don't yell at him, you need to yell at the kid on behalf of the parents. Don't worry about them getting on your case about disciplining their children—they expect and encourage other people to step in when they're too pussy to do it themselves. Occasionally, they might call the police, so when the cops show up, yell at them as well. If they take you to jail, make a scene in your cell and yell at the warden. When you get your day in court, yell at the judge. He'll be so impressed by your vocal fortitude that he'll not only acquit you but also invite you over to have a beer and sex with his wife. If he doesn't invite you, do it anyway, because it was probably his intention.

Show me someone who doesn't yell, and I'll show you a serial killer. Some people are under the impression that yelling is the result of an inability to control your temper. Wrong. An inability to control your temper would be waiting for someone to leave his home, following him to work, running him off the freeway, and bashing his face against the steering column. Yelling keeps your temper in check so that you don't have to resort to excessive violence and gunning down co-workers. You never hear people say "it was that loud motherfucker in the cubicle next to me" when they talk about the people who go postal. It's always the quiet ones. Rather than being stigmatized and reserved for the mentally unstable, yellers should be heralded as champions of good health and mental stability.

YELLING

YELLING GONE WRONG

The most infamous account of yelling gone wrong is exemplified with the Native American battle cry. When enemy troops would attack, the Indians would put their ears to the ground and listen to the horses stampeding toward them. This careful observation was usually the only form of advanced warning that the Indians had.[1] This was in contrast to how the Indians: it was customary for them to yell loud war cries in an attempt to frighten and intimidate their foes. Unfortunately for the Indians, this yelling would instead serve as an advanced warning to their enemies, allowing them to take up arms and prepare for the impending attack long before the battle took place (Figures 1–2). Historians would agree that this strategy was shitty.

Figure 1: Thanks to this . . .   Figure 2: . . . we now have this.

DISCRIMINATION

Although yelling is generally acceptable in any language, there have been a few exceptions in recent years. For example, one time I was on a flight across the Atlantic, and I asked the flight attendant if I could

1. There were also smoke clouds sent by neighboring tribes, which was a great system of communication as long as it wasn't raining, snowing, too windy, or night time.

take a tour of the pilot's cabin. She objected by citing some federal regulations or some other such formality. So I started yelling at her in Arabic because sometimes I like to yell in another language just to change things up a bit.

The next thing I know, these two brutes sitting next to me were trying to get me out of my seat. So I tried to light my shoe on fire so that I could throw it at them, but this only made them crazier. I continued fighting with the passengers sitting next to me until we landed. When the plane finally touched down, the pilot kicked me off and told me I'd have to catch another form of transportation to get home, simply because I yelled in another language.

FAMOUS YELLERS

Sometimes yelling can make people with boring and unremarkable lives famous. Case in point: Paul Revere. Before Revere undertook his celebrated "midnight ride"—a mission to warn militias in his town of approaching British troops—he was by anyone's account a loser. Revere had a modest upbringing and an undistinguished academic career. Legend has it that the headmaster at his school was so fed up with Revere's unrelenting mediocrity that Revere was sent to remedial school, where he spent most of his time producing unremarkable finger paintings, and he had great difficulty keeping his letters between the dotted lines (Figure 3).

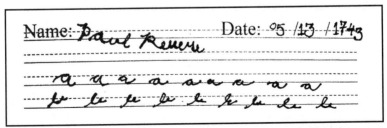

Figure 3: Paul Revere—an unremarkable effort from an unremarkable man.

Fortunately for Revere, his one saving grace was that he was endowed with a powerful set of lungs, which he put to good use during his famous ride as a messenger in the American Revolutionary War. If it weren't for Revere's yelling, today we'd all be eating mango chutney on our pizzas with our crooked yellow teeth.

ONLINE ETIQUETTE

IT'S GENERALLY CONSIDERED RUDE TO TYPE IN CAPS ONLINE BECAUSE IT'S CONSIDERED YELLING. I THINK PEOPLE WHO TYPE IN CAPS ARE BEING COURTEOUS BECAUSE IT MAKES WHAT THEY'RE TYPING EASIER TO READ. I THINK I'LL WRITE THE REST OF THIS BOOK IN CAPS FROM THIS POINT ON. [*No you won't—Editor*]

 **is for...**
ZOMBIES

THERE ARE TWO BASIC TYPES OF ZOMBIES: corpses that have been brought back to life by top-secret biological agents leaked from mishandled army canisters and lifeless corporate drones. I will document the habits and characteristics of the latter type of zombie in this section, as well as the best way to cope should you find yourself confronted by a group of zombies in the workplace.

THE OFFICE ZOMBIE

The North American office zombie's life begins at the early age of five. At five years old, the zombie, still a child, is sent to an entry-level brainwashing institution called "kindergarten." It is in kindergarten that the child is first told that everything he does—every stroke of crayon outside the line, every malformed finger painting, and every piece of construction paper glued to a Popsicle stick—would directly determine his or her social status and financial success. This is done at an early age to create the notion of an absolute authority that wields the power to deny the child his future happiness and to sustain a constant fear of failure.

The child is then "graduated" through different grades, each with a minor distinction, to give the child the illusion of progress. It is during this period that the child first experiences isolation and hostility from other zombie children. An artificial social hierarchy will be created based on a child's perceived popularity and economic standing, which will be strictly enforced by the more popular zombies, and even the authority figures, throughout the subject's entire childhood.

At the age of twelve, the child is ripped from the womb of this institution and thrown into another called "junior high." The child feels rejected and out of place as his body experiences growth in this foreign environment. All the people around him are uncaring and unsympathetic, which makes him feel vulnerable and desperate, causing him to rebel against authority. This rebellion is short lived though, as authority figures swiftly quash the insurgency with prejudice to prevent the other zombies from having their own thoughts of independence.

The frustration of the junior high experience culminates with yet another institution called "high school," where the social hierarchies created in the child's youth are reinforced and the divides are deepened. Any child not yet belonging to a social group is ridiculed until he succumbs to the pressure to conform and joins a group that will accept him, only to be further mocked for joining an unpopular group. After high school, the child, having spent the first part of his life completing menial tasks for the meager approval of arbitrary figureheads, will finally be prepared to enter the workplace to spend the rest of his life completing menial tasks for the meager approval of arbitrary figureheads. But on the bright side, there are casual Fridays.

While most of the students will be ready for their new homes in the office after high school, some of the zombies are coaxed into taking four more years of indoctrination in a place called "college" with promises of getting even more money in the workplace, and by extension, the highest level of happiness.

ON THE JOB

Here's what the office zombie's first day of work looks like:

9:00 AM—The first day starts out optimistically; there's free coffee in the break room, and life is good.

9:03—The calcium deposits in the coffee pot have grown to a considerable size and can now be legally classified as coral reef. Not that it matters because your elder colleagues relish the opportunity for a free cup of anything and make sure to take every last drop of it for themselves every day, hours before you come to work.

9:30—You sit down at your desk and stare in awe at the dust particles glistening in the beams of light, and you wonder how long you could stare off vacantly before anyone notices.

ZOMBIES

10:00—You check your e-mail. No new messages. You lean back in your chair and carve at a hole you've whittled into the side of your desk. You feel proud because it's almost deep enough to fit the tip of your pen inside.

10:20—You wonder why the receptionist waits for three rings before she picks up the phone. You secretly hope for an earthquake to liven things up.

12:00 PM—Lunch is a great opportunity for you to practice avoiding your co-workers.

4:00—Nobody really cares.

5:00—Just before you leave, you receive an e-mail from someone in management who needs an urgent project completed, and there's no way that he could have told you sooner. You have to work uncompensated overtime. Tough shit.

CO-WORKERS

The only thing that could make the cold, calculated corporate facade more abrasive to one's psyche is the addition of inept, loud-mouthed, jackass co-workers. Spending even a few months in a corporate environment will guarantee that you'll encounter at least a few of the following colleagues. Here's a brief list of who to look out for.

THE ASS KISSER: Ass kissers come in two varieties: regular and backstabbing motherfucker. The regular kind of ass kisser is the employee who always sides with the boss during meetings, is on a nickname basis with the

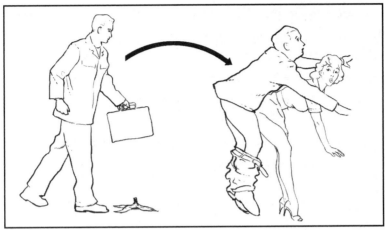

Figure 1: It happens.

boss's son, and always brings cookies that his wife baked for the boss, though it's widely believed that the ass kisser is not married and bakes the cookies himself. Do not mistake this person for a "nice guy." The difference between an ass kisser and a nice guy is that an ass kisser loves to gloat. The reason an ass kisser sucks up so much to authority is not so much that he's ambitious and wants a promotion, as it is that the he thrives on being praised so he can feel distinguished among his co-workers, like the praise you give to a dog for fetching a stick.

The other kind of ass kisser is the backstabbing motherfucker. The primary difference between the two varieties is that unlike the normal ass kisser, the backstabbing motherfucker will go out of his way to get you in trouble. For example, if you accidentally trip and fall with your pants down and have sex with the secretary who also happens to be the boss's daughter (Figure 1), you can be sure the boss will hear it first from the backstabbing motherfucker.

THE SPIRITUAL TEAM LEADER: An overzealous manager who loves "team building" and would be perfectly content to spend the rest of his life in meetings.

This type of manager calls for meetings several times per week to get a chance to use all the new business jargon he's picked up from executive memos and mission statements. Since the spiritual team leader doesn't serve a functional purpose, he constantly feels unsure about his job security and will overcompensate for it by using important sounding words like "actionable," "mindshare," and "turnkey solution" to validate his worth, because the best way to feel important when you're not important is to surround yourself with important-sounding words.

SWAMP FOOT: This office dweller gets his name from the distinct smell of his feet: one part imitation leather, and one part swamp. The only arguably good thing about this odorous colleague is that you can smell him before you see him, giving you a chance to duck into an empty office for a breather.

This is the guy who got the job right out of high school, and in a scramble to look "professional" he went to a clothing store the night before his first day on the job and bought the cheapest dress shirt and slacks that he could find. You can tell that they're his only work clothes because he wears the same set of pants to work every day, occasionally switching up his shirt when the ketchup stains accumulate above the point where he can't tuck his shirt into his pants any deeper.

Not content with just smelling and looking bad, some breeds of swamp foot kick it up a notch by eating Cheetos, Dorritos, or buttered popcorn and then wiping their hands on their pants, leaving behind dark orange and brown streaks as evidence of their nastiness.

THE UNSTABLE JANITOR (AND FAMILY): One of the easiest decisions a corporate head will have to make is in hiring the janitorial service for the office. Since the janitors come in late at night or early in the morning when none of the clients are around, management can cut corners by hiring ex-cons and borderline mental patients to do the work.

The janitor usually brings his extended family to the office so he can put his kids to work to get the job done quicker, but this never goes as smoothly as planned. His kids usually run around screaming while he argues with his wife and becomes increasingly violent, slamming doors and yelling at his vacuum cleaner when it gets unplugged. While the unstable janitor's delusional ranting can be unsettling, he poses no real threat to anyone (assuming you don't make eye contact).

PERPETUAL STINK EYE: He's that one guy in the office who you've never been acquainted with, and yet this guy is your mortal enemy; you have no say in the matter. He hates you with every fiber of his being, and he'll make sure you know it by giving you an eye full of stink every time you walk by. Your attempts to break the ice by saying "hello" to him will fall on deaf ears; he is indifferent to polite greetings and civil discourse.

The only reason anyone can guess as to why he's so bitter is because of the bad divorce he went through over five years ago. He'll sit in his cubicle with a fixed gaze, staring at a picture of his ex-wife, and occasionally crying after he stumbles into work after a night of hard drinking. You can't help but wonder what his job is since he never has any windows open and rarely types anything or talks to anyone. It would be prudent to plan an escape route (and at least one backup) and to learn his work schedule closely so that when he gets fired and takes the office hostage, you can wait in the maintenance closet and sip on piña coladas until the police standoff ends with four hollow-tipped rounds in his chest.

THE POWER-HUNGRY COCK WHORE: Her hunger for power is only rivaled by her hunger for cock. Almost every man in the office will eventually have a fling with the cock whore (and occasionally a few women, if they're high enough in the corporate hierarchy). The only exception is swamp foot, whose sexual frustrations will culminate in an online relationship with an elf from "Ever Quest," who he'll campaign with for several weeks until the server crashes and he never hears from her again, often

ZOMBIES

causing him to think back wistfully at the prospect of almost having a relationship with another humanoid.

The cock whore is the woman all the dirty stories are written about in the men's bathroom. Her inability to get promoted based on her merits lies at the root of her skankiness. Years later, when she's sobbing on the toilet because of the burning sensation she gets when she pees, she'll try to rationalize what she did over the phone to her best friend—who also happens to think she's a slut—by giving a long spiel about how she "has to eat, too" and that the world is unfair to women anyway, and apparently the only way she could succeed was to get her ass hammered up the corporate ladder (either that, or learning how to type without pecking at the keys).

THE PAUPER: Every office has a pauper—someone who constantly complains about not making enough money. Rather than getting off his dead ass, picking up new skills, or working harder, he'll opt to bitch and moan about it instead. Of course, the money he makes is never enough because he keeps pissing it away on sporting events and car stereo equipment to make his obnoxiously loud car even more obnoxiously loud.

What makes the pauper especially annoying is that he will make an envious comment about the things you purchase. If you suggest that he could buy the same, he'll snap back at you with "not all of us make the kind of money you do." He'll usually stop short of suggesting that you don't deserve the money you've earned, but you know it has crossed his mind and that somewhere on the Internet he has posted about it on a forum where his dipshit friends encourage him by saying that he deserves a raise.

FATHER TIME: Father Time is the self-appointed office timekeeper. He's there before everyone else, so if by chance you want to leave early some day, he'll make a snide comment like "must be nice to leave early." At first you think nothing of it, then when you're in your car driving home it hits you:

the sharp sting of sarcasm. Those words, "must be nice," keep resonating in your skull over and over again; with each reverberation, you gain a deeper understanding of his subtle derision—to say that something "must be nice" is to say that (1) it's a luxury and (2) he hasn't experienced this luxury for himself, because if he had, he wouldn't have to contemplate that it must be nice since he would know firsthand that it is, and it's in this moment of clarity that you realize what just happened: He made you his bitch.

The gloves have come off, and your relationship with him from that day forth will no longer be a cordial one. And yet, you cannot confront him about it because it's too late. You didn't catch it fast enough, or maybe you did—it doesn't matter because his comment was passive, and if you confront him, it makes you look like a paranoid asshole. Your only recourse is to stay at work late one day, wait until everyone leaves, then rake your patch on his keyboard (Figure 2).

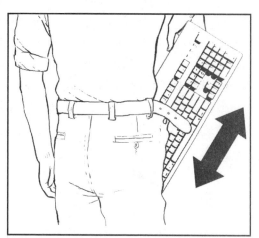

Figure 2: Scratch for justice. Make sure not to make skin contact with the keyboard (herpes, etc.).

THE INCREDIBLE RETRACTING ASSHOLE: Not to be confused with an excretory opening at the end of the pyloric canal, the incredible retracting asshole is the type of person who will tell you what's on his mind, but rather than just saying it, he'll retract his statement by saying "just kidding," even though he's not. He knows what he's saying, and he knows exactly why he's saying it. Although you would enjoy nothing more than to watch this son of a bitch die in his sleep from smoke inhalation, part of you can't help but admire the genius of his technique. This prick has found a way to deliver his payload without any fear of retribution, like a stealth bomber under the cover of night with cloaking technology and camouflage paint and invisibility rays that it can use to shoot itself to become invisible.

DJ DOUCHEMASTER: He's the only guy in the office who refuses to bring headphones to work. Instead, he'll listen to the same shitty album all day long through his desktop speakers, over and over again until you can't take it anymore and you gnaw your own face off. Even if you happen to like the album he's listening to, the songs are constantly interrupted by the chorus of instant messaging buzzes and e-mail alerts that he receives every few seconds so the songs are ruined permanently, and if that wasn't reason enough, the fact that DJ Douchemaster has a similar taste in music should be enough to make you stop listening to the album, if not the entire genre.

Illustrator Index

Angelo Vildasol

Letter E: Main, Fig. 1, 2, 3, 4
Letter N: Main, Fig. 1, 2, 3
Letter S: Main, Fig. 1, 2
Letter X: Main

Bryan Douglas

Letter G: Main, Fig. 1, 2, 3, 4, 5, 6, 7, 8, 9
Letter H: Main
Letter L: Main, Fig. 1, 2, 3
Letter Y: Main, Fig. 1, 2

Jim Moore

Letter U: Main, Fig. 1, 2, 3, 5, 6, 7
Letter Z: Main, Fig. 1, 2

John Petersen

Letter I: Main, Fig. 1, 2, 3
Letter J: Main
Letter P: Main, Fig. 1, 2, 3, 4, 5
Letter R: Main, Fig. 1, 2
Letter V: Fig. 3, 4

Justina Fader

Letter C: Main, Fig. 1, 2, 3, 4, 5, 6, 7, 8, 9, 10
Letter F: Main, Fig. 1, 2, 3, 4, 5
Letter K: Fig. 3, 4, 5, 6, 7

Leah Tiscione

Letter B: Main, Fig. 1, 2, 3, 4, 5, 6, 7, 8
Letter D: Main, Fig. 1
Letter K: Main, Fig. 1, 2
Letter O: Main
Letter T: Main, Fig. 1
Letter W: Main

Louis Fernet-Leclair

Letter M: Main, Fig. 1, 2, 3, 4, 5, 6, 7, 8, 9,
10, 11, 12
Letter V: Main, Fig. 1, 2, 5, 6, 7

Thomas Pollock Jr.

Letter A: Main, Fig. 1, 2, 3, 4, 5, 6, 7, 8, 9, 10,
11, 12, 13, 14
Letter J: Fig. 3
Letter Q: Main
Letter X: Fig. 1, 2, 3, 4

Bob Larkin

Cover Illustration